A Practical Guide to Verilog-A

Mastering the Modeling Language for Analog Devices, Circuits, and Systems

Slobodan Mijalković

Apress®

A Practical Guide to Verilog-A: Mastering the Modeling Language for Analog Devices, Circuits, and Systems

Slobodan Mijalković
The Hague, Zuid-Holland, The Netherlands

ISBN-13 (pbk): 978-1-4842-6350-1   ISBN-13 (electronic): 978-1-4842-6351-8
https://doi.org/10.1007/978-1-4842-6351-8

Managing Director, Apress Media LLC: Welmoed Spahr
Acquisitions Editor: Susan McDermott
Development Editor: James Markham
Coordinating Editor: Jessica Vakili

Distributed to the book trade worldwide by Springer Science+Business Media New York, 233 Spring Street, 6th Floor, New York, NY 10013. Phone 1-800-SPRINGER, fax (201) 348-4505, e-mail orders-ny@springer-sbm.com, or visit www.springeronline.com. Apress Media, LLC is a California LLC and the sole member (owner) is Springer Science + Business Media Finance Inc (SSBM Finance Inc). SSBM Finance Inc is a **Delaware** corporation.

For information on translations, please e-mail booktranslations@springernature.com; for reprint, paperback, or audio rights, please e-mail bookpermissions@springernature.com.

Apress titles may be purchased in bulk for academic, corporate, or promotional use. eBook versions and licenses are also available for most titles. For more information, reference our Print and eBook Bulk Sales web page at http://www.apress.com/bulk-sales.

Any source code or other supplementary material referenced by the author in this book is available to readers on the Github repository: https://github.com/Apress/A-Practical-Guide-to-Verilog-A. For more detailed information, please visit http://www.apress.com/source-code.

Printed on acid-free paper

To

Silva and Jona

Table of Contents

About the Author

Dr. Slobodan Mijalković is a Modeling Scientist and a Senior R&D Engineer at Silvaco, Inc., specialized in semiconductor device modeling for electronic design automation (EDA) software tools. Before joining Silvaco, he was a Principal Researcher in HiTeC Laboratory at the Delft University of Technology in the Netherlands, where he led a team for the standardization of the Mextram bipolar transistor model with Compact Model Coalition (CMC). Formerly, he was an Assistant and an Associate Professor with the Department of Microelectronics at the Faculty of Electronics Engineering, University of Niš, in Serbia (Yugoslavia).

Dr. Mijalković has authored 60 cited publications including 5 book chapters and the monograph *Multigrid Methods for Process Simulation* published by Springer. In the period 2002–2006, he has set and chaired four editions of "Compact Modeling for RF Application (CMRF)" workshops that strongly contributed to the acceptance of Verilog-A as a standard compact modeling language. He is a senior member of IEEE.

About the Technical Reviewer

Massimo Nardone has more than 22 years of experience in security, web/mobile development, and cloud and IT architecture. His true IT passions are security and Android.

He has been programming and teaching how to program with Android, Perl, PHP, Java, VB, Python, C/C++, and MySQL for more than 20 years.

He holds a Master of Science degree in Computing Science from the University of Salerno, Italy.

He has worked as a Project Manager, Software Engineer, Research Engineer, Chief Security Architect, Information Security Manager, PCI/SCADA Auditor, and Senior Lead IT Security/Cloud/SCADA Architect for many years.

Acknowledgments

First, I would like to acknowledge the OVI and Accellera standardization committees for tremendous work in developing and maintaining the Verilog-A language standard over a period of almost 20 years. But also, the Si2 Compact Model Coalition (CMC) for promoting the Verilog-A language since its introduction as the industry standard for compact modeling, in particular Geoffrey Coram and Colin McAndrew, the two Verilog-A gurus and the best guardians of correct Verilog-A usage.

Thanks to everyone on the Apress team for their efforts in bringing this manuscript to the page. Special thanks to the coordinating editor Jessica Vakili, production coordinator Krishnan Sathyamurthy, and project manager Linthaa Muralidharan.

Finally, I thank my parents, family, and friends for their constant support and encouragement. I would like to express special thanks to my fantastic wife, Silva, for professional help, but also for tolerating my incessant disappearances into my home office, during the writing of this book.

Introduction

The digital revolution (also known as the third industrial revolution) made a dramatic shift from analog to digital technology and electronics. In a world that seems dominated by digital information processing, one may wonder if there is still room for analog functions. Of course, it is unwise to assume that analog signal processing will go extinct. Without analog devices, circuits, and systems, digital systems would lack the means for interaction with the physical world. And the need for such interfaces is only growing as we are stepping into the fourth industrial revolution. Technologies like autonomous drive and the Internet of Things increasingly require advanced sensors in various physical domains, improvements in radio frequency communication, and new energy harvesting solutions, all essentially based on analog devices, circuits, and systems.

In the fast-evolving, socially interconnected world, we are witnessing a seismic shift in the amount of data that needs to be processed in real time. Moving forward, the conventional digital processing, with the separation of data and computing, becomes critically constrained by the energy growth of data movement. This will necessitate breaking the barriers of digital abstractions by shifting information representation from symbolic to physically meaningful quantities and switching from sequential discrete-time to continuous-time dynamics. Most of these efforts to revive analog computing borrow essential ideas from natural analog computing processes. These include, but are not limited to, neuromorphic computing, cellular automata, memcomputing, and Ising model–based systems.

For systems consisting wholly of analog components, analog modeling and simulation are essential for checking a system's structural design and for making predictions about the system behavior. But even when the system is partially or fully digital, analog modeling and simulation may still be necessary. Signal integrity properties, such as delays, noise, and distortion, often cannot be disregarded in digital high-speed circuits. Signal integrity analysis of digital circuits and systems is essentially based on analog modeling and simulation.

Analog hardware description language Verilog-A is a particularly suitable framework for design-oriented modeling and simulation of analog devices, circuits, and systems. It applies to both electrical and non-electrical as well as conservative and signal-flow system descriptions. Both the structure and behavior of a multidiscipline analog system can be modeled with Verilog-A on different levels of abstraction. Anything that can be modeled with Verilog-A can also be simulated. Besides, the standard exists for the Verilog-A language, which means that Verilog-A models can be easily exchanged between different simulators.

Verilog-A Language Evolution

The Verilog-A language was introduced in 1996 during the contest between Verilog-HDL and VHDL, the two industry-standard digital hardware description languages (HDLs), to expand into analog and mixed analog-digital applications. The non-profit organization Open Verilog International (OVI), which had standardized Verilog-HDL with IEEE in 1995, took responsibility to define and standardize Verilog-AMS as an analog and mixed-signal extension to Verilog-HDL. The release of the Verilog-A Language Reference Manual (LRM) 1.0 in 1996 as an OVI standard was the first step of that initiative. It was the beginning of the Verilog-A language evolution with basic milestones shown in Figure 1.

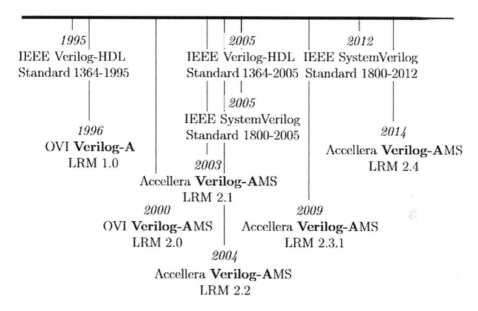

Figure 1. *Timeline of the Verilog-A language evolution*

Following the standardization plan, OVI released the first complete definition of the Verilog-AMS standard in 2000. It was a combination of the IEEE Verilog-HDL standard 1364-1995, the updated OVI Verilog-A standard from 1996, and new language extensions providing mixed-signal modeling features. OVI planned to merge these three parts into a single HDL that would be eventually standardized by IEEE, but it did not happen. Verilog-AMS continued to evolve as a superset to IEEE Verilog-HDL defined by Accellera, the standardization body that succeeded OVI.

Fortunately, Verilog-A did not cease to exist with the birth of Verilog-AMS. After the introduction of the Verilog-A LRM 1.0, it has become clear that there are important applications requiring and benefiting from Verilog-A modeling capabilities. The Verilog-A language has continued to exist and evolve as an all-analog subset of the Verilog-AMS language. A special annex is provided in Verilog-AMS LRMs to help users and compiler developers clearly define Verilog-A within the Verilog-AMS language. In the process of standardization, Verilog-AMS experienced several major

LRM revisions with each new LRM revision superseding the syntax and semantics of the previous ones. Numerous language enhancements have been introduced as well as various modifications required to resolve conflicts with the independently developing IEEE Verilog-HDL standard. Most of these enhancements and modifications also affected the syntax and semantics of the analog-only subset Verilog-A.

In 2005, the IEEE Verilog-HDL was rolled into a newly introduced hardware description and verification language SystemVerilog. Accellera responded by releasing Verilog-AMS LRM 2.4 in 2014 as the final version of this standard and decided to focus on defining SystemVerilog-AMS as an analog and mixed-signal extension to SystemVerilog. Nevertheless, Verilog-AMS started adopting some of the SystemVerilog language features starting from LRM 2.3, affecting also to some extent the Verilog-A syntax and semantics. At the time this book was written, the SystemVerilog-AMS standard was not yet introduced, but it is already announced that Verilog-A will be preserved as an analog-only subset also within the SystemVerilogh-AMS language.

Verilog-A and SPICE-like Simulators

The Verilog-A language was introduced with two basic objectives. The first one was to define an analog HDL with similar syntax and related semantics to digital Verilog-HDL as a subset of Verilog-AMS. The other objective was to provide compatibility of Verilog-A with the SPICE simulation engine.

SPICE (Simulation Program with Integrated Circuit Emphasis) was developed at the University of California at Berkeley in 1971 as a tool to predict analog circuit behavior from circuit connectivity and analytical models of circuit components. The birth and growth of the integrated circuit industry in the 1970s led to the widespread adoption of the Berkeley SPICE program. Furthermore, the availability of the SPICE code and documentation from Berkeley, for a nominal fee, spurred the development of SPICE-like simulators in academia, industry, and commercial products.

Today, there are thousands of copies of SPICE-like circuit simulators in use across academia and industry, and there are many commercial SPICE-like simulators in the market.

All major commercial SPICE-like simulators support also the Verilog-A language. The compatibility with the SPICE simulation engine was not the only reason for the widespread adoption of Verilog-A in SPICE-like simulators. Verilog-A was able to expand SPICE modeling and simulation capabilities both in the level of abstraction and domain of application, as it is schematically shown in Figure 2.

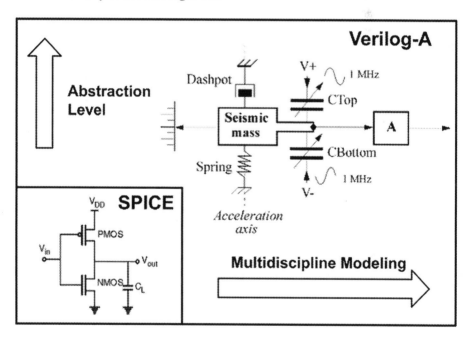

Figure 2. *SPICE and Verilog-A application domains*

With the syntactic heritage from Verilog-HDL and semantics derived from SPICE fundamentals, Verilog-A can effectively describe analog behavior at both system high level and SPICE circuit level of abstraction. It allows for the top-down analog design, where the starting point could be a system described in the form of block or signal-flow diagrams, which is successively partitioned and refined until the detailed SPICE circuit–level implementation is obtained.

On the other hand, Verilog-A extends SPICE with multidiscipline modeling capabilities. In addition to electrical discipline, being a traditional SPICE modeling domain, Verilog-A supports other energy domains such as magnetic, thermal, or kinematic, with the possibility to define additional custom disciplines. With Verilog-A, the models from different disciplines and abstraction levels can be freely mixed in the same analog design.

Verilog-A and Compact Modeling

SPICE circuit element models are commonly referred to as compact models. They should be sufficiently simple to provide efficient circuit simulation and sufficiently accurate to make the outcome of the simulation useful to circuit designers.

Compact models were traditionally hand-coded in C, including derivatives of the model expressions, and tightly intertwined with SPICE solver algorithms. With continuous advances in device and circuit technology, the number and complexity of compact models increased dramatically, producing a burden on new compact model implementation. As other SPICE-like simulators emerged, with different data structures and solver algorithms, compact models had to be hand-implemented multiple times; see Figure 3.

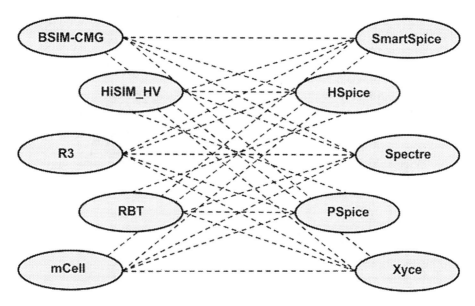

Figure 3. *Implementing every model in every SPICE-like simulator*

The obvious solution to the issue of implementing every model in every simulator was to completely separate compact model code from the simulator code. With Verilog-A, the code of compact models has changed from being tightly integrated within simulators to being defined in a stand-alone manner, as demonstrated in Figure 4.

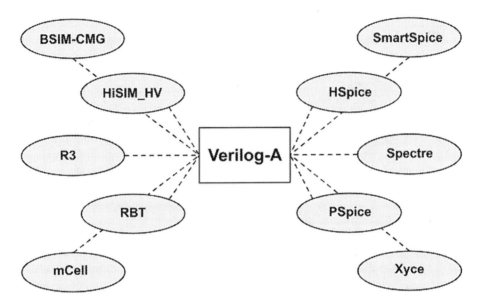

Figure 4. *Separating compact models from SPICE-like simulators*

With the introduction of language extensions to support compact device modeling in LRM 2.2, Verilog-A has become the de facto standard language in the electronics industry for coding compact models of active and passive semiconductor devices. All industry-standard compact models released by Si2 Compact Model Coalition[1] (CMC) as well as compact models of emerging nano-electronics devices released by the New Era Electronic Devices and Systems[2] (NEEDS) initiative are coded in Verilog-A.

---

[1] https://si2.org/cmc/
[2] https://nanohub.org/groups/needs/compact_models

Verilog-A Fundamentals

A general multidiscipline analog system is described in Verilog-A using a lumped-component model. It simplifies the description of a spatially distributed physical system into a topology of interconnected components which are acted upon by a stimulus and produce a response. Verilog-A provides modeling constructs for both structure and behavior of the lumped-component system description.

Elements of Structure

Verilog-A permits the hierarchical description of a system structure. It allows the decomposition of a complex system into a set of smaller manageable subsystems, being possibly further recursively decomposed up to any appropriate level of deepness. The hierarchical system partitioning is based on *modules*. The top-level module represents the system under consideration. A hierarchical description is created when higher-level modules create instances of lower-level modules, as schematically shown in Figure 5.

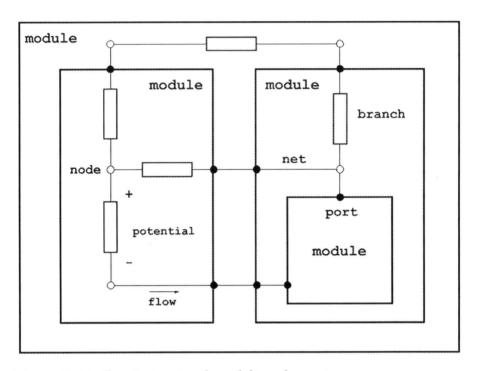

Figure 5. *Verilog-A structural modeling elements*

A lumped-component model is implemented in Verilog-A instantiating
two-terminal components, or *branches*, within modules. The branch
terminals are interconnected by *nets* which are hierarchically extended
through module *ports*. Nets are topological abstractions of physical
links among system components which make the physical position and
geometry of modules and branches irrelevant. Each port is associated with
two nets, a net in the instantiating module, or upper connection, and a net
in the instantiated module, or lower connection. The lower and upper port
connections are also known as formal and actual module connectors.

A net provides connectivity within a module when it is used as
a branch terminal or port connector. Module ports extend the net
connectivity of branch terminals to upper or lower levels of the module
hierarchy. In that way, the connectivity of branch terminals can traverse

the module hierarchy. A junction where two or more branch terminals hierarchically connect is called a *node*. It allows us to consider system structure as a network of branches with terminals connected to nodes. The lumped network is drawn as a collection of nodes and branches. A node is a point of interconnection for the branches, and a branch is a path between two nodes. As such, a branch always has two terminals and each terminal connects to one node.

Elements of Behavior

A unifying concept to describe the behavior of a wide range of general multidiscipline lumped-component systems is energy. The system components may thus be thought of as energy manipulators which process the energy injected into the system depending upon the way they are interconnected.

In Verilog-A, each net is declared as a data object of a net-discipline type to define a domain in which the net supports energy exchange in the system. The net-discipline types are defined by *flow* and *potential*, a pair of physical quantities associated with the *natures* of energy exchange among system components. The flow is an intensive quantity, typically representing energy flux or power, like electrical current or mechanical force. On the other hand, the potential is an extensive quantity that gives the pitch of the energy flow, like electrical voltage or mechanical pressure. The product of flow and potential physically represents the energy or instantaneous power.

Branches and nodes are the model objects that carry the flow and potential quantities. A branch is a path of flow between two nodes. All branch terminal nets connected to a node share the same potential. The potential of the node is in that way shared with all continuous hierarchical nets connected via ports to the node. The branch terminals share the same flow which is also the flow through the branch. The difference between potentials in nodes connected by a branch is a *branch potential*. While nodal potentials are defined relative to the global reference (or *ground*) potential, branch potentials are independent of the global potential reference. A product of the branch potential and the flow through the branch corresponds to the instantaneous power (or energy) being exchanged with the branch. The nodal potentials and flow in branches define the system state and behavior at any instance of time. They are also commonly referred to as system *signals*.

The behavior of a circuit is captured in Verilog-A by two sets of relationships for nodal potentials and branch flows. The first set of relationships is implicitly defined by the system network interconnections using the General Kirchhoff Potential Law (GPL) and the General Kirchhoff Flow Law (GFL). GFL and GPL state that the flow from all branches at a node and the sum of all branch potentials around a loop of connected branches shall sum to zero at any instant of time. These are essentially Kirchhoff's laws for electrical circuits generalized to any energy domain associated with the net-disciplines. The second set of relationships is the branch constitutive relationships. They are explicitly introduced in a Verilog-A code by branch contribution statements defining each branch flow or potential in terms of other potential and flow variables in the system. The nature of nets may be abstracted either as directional signal flows or as satisfying conservative-law relationships between quantities. Conservative-law relationships assume the existence of both branch flow and potential.

Compilation and Simulation

One of the main motivations for writing a model of an analog system in the Verilog-A language is to enable us to simulate it. The simulation is based on the executable model produced from the Verilog-A code by *analysis* and *elaboration*. The combined analysis and elaboration process is commonly referred to as *compilation*.

The analysis is the process of reading and analyzing Verilog-A source code for lexical, syntactic, and semantic errors. From the source code, the lexical analysis produces tokens, the words in a language, which are then parsed to produce a syntax tree. It is first used to check if code conforms to the syntax rules of a language. Semantic analysis is then performed on the syntax tree to check aspects that are not related to the syntactic form or that are not easily determined during parsing. Compilers may execute compilation in one or more passes saving the compiled results in intermediate formats or passing the compiled results directly to an elaboration phase.

Elaboration is the process of binding together the components that make up a Verilog-A executable model. Elaboration occurs after the compilation phase and before simulation and it involves expanding module instantiations, computing parameter values, resolving hierarchical names, establishing net connectivity, and in general preparing the design for simulation. Some of the Verilog-A statements are used to control the elaboration process. The executable Verilog-A model is defined as a set of continuous-time differential-algebraic equations (DAEs) that come from the behavioral description of the analog system and its signal-flow or conservative-law connection semantics.

The simulation of Verilog-A executable models is based on a time discretization of continuous-time DAEs using discrete time-stepping integration methods and the solution of resulting nonlinear algebraic equations. The quality of the solution depends on tolerances that define the discretization time step and other characteristic values related to the numerical techniques used to solve the system of nonlinear algebraic equations at each time point. Another important characteristic of the simulation of continuous-time models is that a consistent initial (quiescent) operating point is required. Without it, inaccuracies or non-convergence issues could arise during the rest of the simulation.

About This Book

The main intention of this book is to provide a practical guide to the Verilog-A language in its latest standard formulation. There is no doubt that the Accellera Verilog-AMS Language Reference Manual[3] provides the most complete description of the Verilog-A(MS) language standard. However, it is a definitional document written in a complex legalistic style. This makes it difficult to use as a tutorial to learn the Verilog-A language or as a guide when solving practical problems that arise in coding Verilog-A models.

The similar goal of providing a more practical description of the Verilog-A(MS) language than the official LRM description has been already attained by two good books.[4,5] The book by FitzPatrick and Miller, from 1998, is based on the initial Verilog-A LRM 1.0. However, substantial extensions and modifications of the Verilog-A language on the way from LRM 1.0 to LRM 2.4 made this book quite outdated. The other book, by Kundert and Zinke, describes Verilog-AMS (including the Verilog-A language as the all-analog subset) as based on the more recent LRM 2.1, which makes it to a lesser extent outdated. Nevertheless, it is still missing many important language extensions and features introduced after LRM 2.1 and focuses mainly on mixed-signal hardware description capabilities of the Verilog-AMS language. This book is again fully dedicated to the Verilog-A language, as the book from FitzPatrick and Miller, but based on the latest LRM 2.4 description. While the author has worked diligently to ensure that this book provides accurate and complete descriptions of the

---

[3] Verilog-AMS Language Reference Manual (LRM), Version 2.4.0, Accellera Systems Initiative, May 30, 2014.

[4] D. FitzPatrick and I. Miller, Analog Behavioral Modeling with the Verilog-A Language, Springer, 1998.

[5] K. Kundert and O. Zinke, The Designer's Guide to Verilog-AMS, The Designer's Guide Book Series, Springer, 2004.

Verilog-A language, the final authority here remains to be the Accellera Verilog-AMS LRM 2.4 manual.

The book is organized into 20 chapters introduced in a manner that builds foundational knowledge first before moving into more complex topics. No prior knowledge of any hardware description language is assumed and the approach is to learn through relevant examples. This book could be useful to both a newcomer to the Verilog-A language as well as an experienced user who wants to refresh on a certain topic.

CHAPTER 1

Lexical Basis

The most basic study of any language is lexical. Without knowing the rules for constructing words, we cannot begin to write books or even construct a single sentence. Likewise, before we can write a meaningful Verilog-A code, we must learn the rules for constructing words or, more correctly, lexical tokens.

Character Set and Tokens

A Verilog-A source text consists of one or more source files that contain a series of characters. The permissible characters in the Verilog-A source files are shown in Table 1-1.

Table 1-1. *Permissible characters in the Verilog-A language*

Character Name	Symbols
Letters	A B C D ... X Y Z
	a b c d ... x y z
Digits	0 1 2 3 4 5 6 7 8 9
Graphic characters	! " # % & ` ' ( ) * +
	, - . / : ; < = > ? $
	[\ ] ^ _ { | } ~ @
Whitespace characters	Space tab newline form-feed

S. Mijalković, *A Practical Guide to Verilog-A*, https://doi.org/10.1007/978-1-4842-6351-8_1

1

The source character set includes 52 upper- and lowercase letters of the Latin alphabet, 10 decimal digits, 32 special graphic characters, and 4 non-printing or whitespace characters. The non-printing characters do not correspond to visible marks, but typically do occupy an area in the source text.

During lexical analysis, the Verilog-A compiler resolves the stream of characters from the source text into a series of tokens consisting of one or more characters. The tokens in the Verilog-A language could be classified as

- Comments
- Identifiers
- Reserved words
- System names
- Compiler directives
- Numeric literals
- String literals
- Operators
- Punctuators

The whitespace characters serve as token separators and they are not allowed in any token except in string literals. The token separation is provided also with other tokens, like operators and punctuators, but separation by whitespace characters is often necessary to avoid ambiguities. In principle, any whitespace that occurs between tokens is ignored during lexical analysis, except when a whitespace character serves as a token separator.

Comments

Comments are inserted in Verilog-A code for readability and documentation. It is an essential feature of a good coding practice.

The Verilog-A language has two forms to introduce comments. Two forward slashes, //, indicate the start of a one-line comment, which continues until the end of the line:

```
// This is a comment
x=1; // The first part of the line is not a comment
```

An alternative technique is to use block comments which start with /* and end with */. Such comments can continue over many lines:

```
/* This is a comment */
/* This
is
a
longer
comment */
```

Spaces are not allowed within the two forward slashes or between / and * characters:

```
/ * This is not a valid comment * /
/ / Neither is this
```

Two forward slashes // shall not have any special meaning inside a block comment:

```
/* This is a comment with // as a comment text
   and this is a continuation */
```

Block comments shall not be nested:

```
/* /* This comment should
     not pass a Verilog-A lexical analysis */ */
```

3

Since the comments are not relevant as tokens after lexical analysis, each comment is replaced after resolution by a single space character. Because of that, comments are often considered a kind of whitespace.

Identifiers

An identifier is a user-defined token that is introduced to give an object a unique name so it can be referenced in the Verilog-A code. Identifiers are case sensitive; both upper- and lowercase characters in identifiers are valid and distinct.

Note   A good coding practice is to use mainly lowercase identifiers with meaningful names. This makes Verilog-A code easily readable and self-documented.

Verilog-A compilers may set a limit on the maximum length of identifiers, but it should be at least 1024 characters. If an identifier exceeds the specified length limit, an error shall be reported.

An identifier in Verilog-A shall either be a simple identifier or an escaped identifier. Every identifier in Verilog-A has a unique hierarchical name.

Simple Identifiers

A simple identifier is a sequence of some combination of letters, digits, dollar signs ($), and the underscore (_) characters. The first character of a simple identifier shall not be a digit or a dollar sign ($). Examples of valid simple identifiers are

```
initial_velocity
level_1
```

```
merge_ab
_position
n$999
```

whereas invalid simple identifiers include

```
5velocity // Identifier cannot start with a digit
level-1 // Don't confuse - with _
$n999 // Identifier cannot start with $
```

Simple identifiers can have a leading underscore. However, it is best to avoid them, since the leading underscores are often generated and used internally by compilers.

Escaped Identifiers

An escaped identifier starts with the backslash character (\) and ends with a whitespace character. It provides means of including any of the printable ASCII characters (a letter, digit, or graphic character) in an identifier. Examples of valid escaped identifiers are

```
\5$+$velocity
\level-1
\***water-temperature***
\net1/\net2
\{a,b}
\a*(b+c)
```

Neither the leading backslash character nor the terminating whitespace is considered to be part of the identifier. Therefore, an escaped identifier \charge1 is treated the same as a non-escaped identifier charge1.

Hierarchical Names

A hierarchical name is used as a reference to access an identifier in various objects in the Verilog-A code hierarchically. It is specified by concatenating the names of the unilaterally inclusive hierarchical instances up to the instance that locally contains the identifier. The period character (`.`) is used to separate instance names in the hierarchy. For example:

```
u1.struct1.field // u1 must be visible locally
```

is a hierarchical name for the `field` identifier, defined in the instance `struct1` which is instantiated in the framework of `u1`. The system name `$root` refers to the top of the instantiated design:

```
$root.mymodule.u1 // absolute name
```

Both simple and escaped identifiers can be used as hierarchical instance names.

An instance name can be also indexed by introducing the index number in brackets after the instance identifier:

```
field[5].sum
```

The index number is an integer literal (or expression that evaluates a constant integer number). In that way, multiple hierarchical instances can share the same name.

Reserved Words

Reserved words are similar to simple identifiers, with the restriction to use only lowercase letter characters. The reserved words cannot be used as simple identifiers. However, a reserved word preceded by the backslash character becomes an escaped identifier and is not interpreted anymore as a reserved word.

Some of the reserved words in Verilog-A are keywords. Keywords have a special meaning in the Verilog-A language and they are part of the syntax defining various language constructs. The reserved words which are not keywords have no meaning in the Verilog-A code but still it is not allowed to use them as simple identifiers. They are reserved for use in other languages from the Verilog family, such as Verilog-HDL or mixed-signal extension in Verilog-AMS. The complete list of reserved words and keywords in Verilog-A is given in the Appendix.

System Names

A name following the dollar sign ($) character is interpreted as a system name, which can represent a system task or a system function:

```
$finish;
$display ("display a message");
```

The $ character in a system name shall not be followed by a whitespace character and shall not be escaped. Any valid identifier already used in contexts other than this construct, as well as any of the reserved words, can be used as a system name.

The Verilog-A language defines a standard set of system names which will be introduced in the chapters describing corresponding system tasks and functions. The simulator can provide additional system names but they will not be part of the Verilog-A standard.

Compiler Directives

The tokens starting with the open quote (or accent grave) character (`` ` ``) introduce a language construct used to implement compiler directives:

```
`define  M_PI 3.14159265358979323846
```

Verilog-A defines a standard set of compiler directives:

	`define	`undef
`default_transition	`else	`endif
`ifdef	`ifndef	`include
`elsif		

The practical usage of standard compiler directives is described in Chapter 20.

Compiler implementations can also specify additional compiler directives, which may be simulator specific, but not part of the Verilog-A standard. Any valid identifier already in use in contexts other than this construct, as well as any reserved word, can be used as a compiler directive name.

Numerical Literals

A numerical literal is a token that directly denotes a constant numeric value rather than referring to it by name or using some other evaluation rule. The Verilog-A language recognizes integer and real numerical literals.

Integer Literals

Integer literals can be specified in decimal, hexadecimal, octal, or binary formats. They are composed of up to three tokens.

The first and optional token is a nonzero decimal number that specifies the size of the integer literal in terms of its exact number of bits. The second token, a base format, is used to annotate the format and intended usage of integer literals. The base format tokens for different integer literal formats are given in Table 1-2.

Table 1-2. *The base format tokens for integer literals*

Integer Literal Type	Tokens
Decimal	'd 'D 'sd 'Sd 'sD 'sD
Hexadecimal	'h 'H 'sh 'Sh 'sH 'sH
Octal	'o 'O 'so 'So 'sO 'sO
Binary	'b 'B 'sb 'Sb 'sB 'sB

All base format tokens start with the apostrophe (or acute accent) character ('), followed by the optional single character s to indicate a signed quantity, and a letter d, h, o, or b, specifying the base for the number. All the letters are case insensitive and therefore 'sb 'sB 'Sb and 'SB are considered identical tokens. The numbers specified with the base format shall be treated as signed integers if the s designator is included or as unsigned integers if the base format only is used. The s designator does not affect the bit pattern, only its interpretation. If the size of the unsigned number is smaller than the size specified for the literal integer, the unsigned number shall be padded to the left with zeros.

The third token defines the value of an integer literal being a sequence of characters that represent the corresponding numerical system base as shown in Table 1-3.

Table 1-3. *Characters for representation of integer literal values*

Integer Literal Type	Symbols
Decimal	0 1 2 3 4 5 6 7 8 9
Hexadecimal	0 1 2 3 4 5 6 7 8 9 a b c d e f A B C D E F
Octal	0 1 2 3 4 5 6 7
Binary	0 1

Here are some examples of valid and illegal integer literals:

```
4'b1001 // is a 4-bit binary number
5 'D 3 // is a 5-bit decimal number
'h 837FF // is a hexadecimal number
'o7460 // is an octal number
4af // is illegal (hexadecimal format requires 'h)
```

The format token is optional for decimal integer literal. They can be used without the size and the base format as simple decimal integer literals specified as a sequence of digits 0 through 9 without embedded spaces. For example:

```
15984
```

is a valid integer literal in the simple decimal number form but

```
15 984 // Embedded space is not allowed
```

is not. Simple decimal integer literals shall be treated as signed integers. The simple decimal literals are also the most commonly used format for integer literals in Verilog-A code.

The underscore character (_) is legal to use anywhere within the sequence of characters defining integer literal value, except as the first character:

```
27_195_000
32 'h 12ab_f001
_15984 // This is an identifier
```

The underscore characters in the integer literal value tokens are ignored by the Verilog-A compiler. But this feature can be used to break up long numbers for readability purposes.

A plus or minus sign between the base format and the number is illegal syntax. Negative integer literals, if required, shall be represented in two's complement form. A plus or minus sign preceding an integer literal, as in the example:

```
-15984 // This is an integer expression
```

is an integer expression rather than an integer literal.

Real Literals

A real literal is represented by two sequences of decimal digits (integral and fractional) separated with a decimal point (.):

```
1.2
0.1
2394.26331
```

or with an additional exponent part:

```
1.2E12
1.30e-2 // The exponent symbol can be e or E
0.1e-0
```

The exponent part consists of an optional + or – sign followed by an integer literal representing a decimal exponent. The value of the real literal is obtained by multiplying the pre-exponent decimal number by the number 10 raised to the power of decimal exponent.

Real literals shall have at least one digit on each side of the decimal point. The following are invalid forms of real numbers because they do not have at least one digit on each side of the decimal point:

```
.12
9.
4.E3
.2e-7
```

A scale factor can be used instead of the exponent part:

```
2.5001K
25001k
```

No space is permitted between the number and the scale symbol. Table 1-4 describes each of the available scale factor symbols and their value used in scaled notation.

Table 1-4. *Scale symbols and values*

Symbol	Value
T	10^{12}
G	10^{9}
M	10^{6}
K	10^{3}
m	10^{-3}
u	10^{-6}
n	10^{-9}
p	10^{-12}
f	10^{-15}
a	10^{-18}

The underscore character is legal anywhere in a real literal except as the first character of the literal or the first character after the decimal point:

```
236.123_763_e-12 // Identical to 236.123763e-12
_236.123_763_e-12 // An identifier
236._123_763_e-12 // Not legal
```

A plus or minus sign preceding a real literal, as in the example:

`-2.5001e3`

is a constant expression obtained as a combination of the unary operator (in this case `-`) and a real literal.

String Literals

A string literal is a sequence of characters enclosed by the double quote character (") and contained on a single line. The whitespace characters are significant in string literals:

`"Hello world" // Not the same as "Helloworld"`

Notice that the double quote (") is a single character rather than two successive accent characters.

Certain characters are represented in string literals using escape sequences, starting with a backslash character (\). For example, \n signifies a new line, which cannot be otherwise introduced in a string literal contained on a single line. Table 1-5 lists escape sequences that are available to be used in Verilog-A string literals.

Table 1-5. *Escape sequences in Verilog-A string literals*

Escape String	Character Produced by Escape String
\n	Newline character
\t	Tab character
\\	\ character
\"	" character
\o \oo \ooo	Character specified with octal numbers ($0 \leq o \leq 7$)

Note that the octal escape sequence consists of the backslash character (\) followed by one, two, or three octal digits (o). The octal escape sequence ends when it either contains three octal digits already or the next character is not an octal digit.

Operators

An operator is a language feature, represented by a single or double character token, which instructs to perform some well-defined action. The symbols for the Verilog-A operators are similar to those in the C programming language. A complete list of tokens that serve as Verilog-A operators is given in Table 1-6.

Table 1-6. *Verilog-A operator tokens*

Unary Operator	Binary Operator	Operator Type
– +	+ – * / ** %	Arithmetic
	< <= > >= == !=	Relational
!	&& ||	Logical
~	& | ^ ^~ ~^ << >>	Bitwise

Unary operators shall appear to the left of their operand. Binary operators shall appear between their operands. The whitespace is not allowed within the double character operator tokens, meaning, for instance, that * * is not a valid operator.

Besides the operators defined by single tokens, there are additional Verilog-A operators defined by punctuators.

Punctuators

The punctuators in Verilog-A are single or double character tokens that have independent syntactic and semantic meaning to the compiler. Table 1-7 presents all punctuators of the Verilog-A language with the description of their syntactic roles.

Table 1-7. *Verilog-A punctuators*

Punctuators	Role
( )	Grouping, call operator
{ }	Concatenation operator
'{ }	Assignment pattern
[ ]	Range, subscript operator
(* *)	Attribute instances
? :	Conditional operator
;	Statement separator
,	List separator
=	Procedural and attribute assignments
<+	Direct branch contribution
==	Indirect branch contribution
@	Event designator
#	Parameter instantiation designator
:	Block name and range separator
.	Hierarchical names

Some of the punctuators always appear in pairs as shown in the first six rows of Table 1-7.

The role of punctuators in Verilog-A code could be grouping, separation, and designation of other language constructs. In some cases, punctuators take a role of an operator, as is the case of the call, concatenation, subscript, and conditional operators.

Now that we are equipped with the Verilog-A vocabulary, we are ready to start building the first Verilog-A sentences in the form of basic type expressions described in the next chapter.

CHAPTER 2

Basic Types and Expressions

Verilog-A is a typed language. The type of an object in Verilog-A code determines its storage size, the set of values it can have, and what operations can be performed on it. This chapter introduces Verilog-A basic types. Expressions combine basic type objects using operators to produce new basic type values. They serve as building blocks of all data manipulation in a Verilog-A code.

Basic Types

There are three basic types in the Verilog-A language: integer, real, and string types. While the types of integer, real, and string literals are implicitly defined, the type of identifiers referring to basic type values in Verilog-A has to be declared before these identifiers are used in expressions.

Integer Types

The integer type represents a range of integral numbers which can be both positive and negative. An integral number is colloquially defined as a number that can be written without a fractional component.

© Slobodan Mijalković 2022
S. Mijalković, *A Practical Guide to Verilog-A*, https://doi.org/10.1007/978-1-4842-6351-8_2

The integer types are stored using 32-bit words. The signed integer numbers that can be represented in this way range from -2^{31} to $2^{31}-1$, that is, from $-2\_147\_483\_648$ to $2\_147\_483\_647$. The negative integers are represented via *two's complement*. It means that a negative integer $-y$, where $0 \leq y \leq 2^{31}-1$, is stored as a binary representation of the positive integer $2^{32}-y$.

Real Types

The real types are stored as 64-bit words following the IEEE Standard STD-754-1985 for double-precision floating-point numbers as shown in Figure 2-1.

Figure 2-1. *The storage format for a 64-bit real type in Verilog-A*

In the 64-bit IEEE format, a single bit (S) is allocated as the sign bit (0 or 1). The 11 bits in the exponent field (E) provide the maximum exponent range from -1022 to 1023. It defines the value range of the real type. The smallest positive number that can be represented in this way is $2^{-1022}=2.23\times10^{-308}$, while the largest number is $2^{1023}=1.80\times10^{308}$. The precision of the real type is determined by the number of bits in the fraction field (F). The 52 bits in the fractional field correspond to approximately 16 significant decimal digits.

A real number in mathematics assumes a value of a continuous quantity. On the other hand, the real type numbers in Verilog-A can have only a finite subset of all real numbers between the largest and smallest values. A commonly used measure for the gap between discrete real type number values is the *machine epsilon*. It is defined as a gap between the smallest real type number greater than 1 and 1, which is $2^{-52} \approx 2.2 \times 10^{-16}$. In numerical computations, it is very easy to attempt to generate a number whose absolute magnitude is too big to be represented (causing floating-point overflow) or too small (causing floating-point underflow). Subtracting two nearly equal real type values could result in catastrophic cancellation and complete loss of accuracy. One should always keep in mind that the real type numbers are not the exact representation of the real numbers in mathematics.

String Types

The string type in Verilog-A represents an ordered collection of characters. The length of a string variable is defined by the number of characters stored in the string type. There is no limit on the string size, so you do not have to worry about running out of space to store the string. Strings use dynamic memory allocation as their length may vary during simulation.

String types are implemented as bit arrays of a width that is a multiple of 8 bits that hold ASCII values, that is, an individual ASCII character is defined by 8 bits.

Note   Unlike the C programming language, there is no null character \0 at the end of a Verilog-A string, and any attempt to use the null character is ignored.

The string types in Verilog-A can take on the special value " ", which is the empty string.

Expressions

An expression is a formula in which operands are linked to each other by the use of operators to compute a value of a basic type. Expressions can also serve as operands and can be joined together by operators into more complex expressions.

Primary Expressions

Primary expressions are the building blocks of more complex expressions. The simple primary expressions are basic type literals and identifiers declared as references to basic type values. More elaborate primary expressions are call and subscript expressions.

Call Expressions

A call expression in Verilog-A is passing control and arguments (if any) to a function that returns a basic type value.

A call expression is formed by a function name followed by the call operator introduced with parentheses ( ) containing a comma-separated list of call arguments:

```
hypot(arg1, arg2)
maxValue(val1, val2)
idtmod(freq, 0.0, 1.0, -0.5)
$rdist_normal(2, 0, 5n, "instance")
```

The function name is an identifier for the user-defined and signal access functions. It could be also a keyword or system name for built-in functions and analog operators. Any expression can be specified as an argument in a function call but the number and the type of call arguments must agree with the argument declaration in the function definition. Only signal access functions can take a variable number of arguments, one or two net-discipline type identifiers:

```
V(p, n)
V(d)
```

The function argument lists for the user-defined functions should contain at least one argument, while some of the system built-in functions can be used without arguments:

```
$random()
$temperature
```

with the optional use of empty parentheses.

Subscript Expressions

A subscript operator [ ] can be used to access the elements of an array of basic types. One of the two operands in a subscript expression is an array variable name that must precede the brackets. The other, specified within the brackets, is the index value that must be an expression of the integer type:

```
in_val[5]
```

The subscript operator can be applied recursively to access the values in multidimensional arrays:

```
x[n1][n2][n3]
```

The subscript expressions are associated from left to right. The leftmost subscript operator is evaluated first.

Arithmetic Expressions

The operands of the arithmetic expressions may be of real or integer type. The arithmetic operators supported by the Verilog-A language are shown in Table 2-1.

Table 2-1. *The arithmetic operators*

Operator	Meaning	Example	Result
+	Addition	x + y	Sum of x and y
-	Subtraction	x - y	Difference of x and y
*	Multiplication	x * y	Product of x and y
/	Division	x / y	Quotient of x by y
**	Power	x ** y	x to the power of y
%	Modulus	x % y	Remainder of x / y
+(unary)	Positive sign	+ x	Value of x
-(unary)	Negative sign	- x	Arithmetic negation of x

The result of the division operator, /, with integer operands is also an integer obtained as the algebraic quotient with any fractional part discarded. For example, the expressions 5/2 and -5/2 are evaluated as 2 and -2, respectively. For positive quotient, the output is the greatest integer less than or equal to the quotient (floor function of the quotient), while for the negative quotient it is the least integer greater than or equal to the quotient (ceiling function of the quotient).

The modulus expression x % y finds the remainder after division x / y. If both operands are integers, the result is equivalent to the expression:

x - (x / y) * y

For the case where either argument is real, the expression x % y is evaluated as

```
x - ceil(x / y) * y
```

if x/y is negative and

```
x - floor(x / y) * y
```

otherwise. Here, `floor()` and `ceil()` are Verilog-A built-in floor and ceiling functions, respectively.

For mixed real and integer operands, the integer operand is converted to real:

```
1 + 3.145 // is equivalent to 1.0 + 3.145
```

Such implicit type conversions can often be avoided.

Relational Expressions

An expression created using a relational operator forms a relational expression or a condition. The six operators which can be used to form relational expressions are shown in Table 2-2.

Table 2-2. *The relational operators*

Operator	Meaning	Example	Result: 1 (True) or 0 (False)
<	Less than	x < y	1 if x is less than y
<=	Less than or equal to	x <= y	1 if x is less than or equal to y
>	Greater than	x > y	1 if x is greater than y
>=	Greater than or equal to	x >= y	1 if x is greater than or equal to y
==	Equal to	x == y	1 if x is equal to y
!=	Not equal to	x != y	1 if x is not equal to y. In all other cases, the result is 0

A comparison of the left and right operands is carried out and the result is either true or false. Since there is no boolean type in Verilog-A, the integer type is used to represent true or false. Relational expressions return 0 or 1, where 0 stands for false and 1 stands for true.

You can also compare strings with relational expressions. Both operands can be of type string, or one of them can be a string literal which is implicitly converted to a string type for the comparison. The integer value of each character of the left string operand is compared to the integer value of each character of the right string operand working from left to right.

Logical Expressions

The operands can be of the real or integer type. The three logical operators in Verilog-A are shown in Table 2-3.

Table 2-3. *The logical operators*

Operator	Meaning	Example	Result: 1 (True) or 0 (False)
&&	Logical AND	x && y	1 if both x and y are not equal to 0
||	Logical OR	x || y	1 if either of both x and y is not equal to 0
!	Logical NOT	!x	1 if x equals 0. In all other cases, the result is 0

Logical operators evaluate each operand in terms of its equivalence to 0. The result of a logical expression is the integer with a value of 0 or 1.

Bitwise Expressions

The bitwise expressions are concerned with the operations on single bits of integer types. There are seven bitwise operators, five logical and two shift bitwise operators, as described in Table 2-4.

Table 2-4. *The bitwise operators*

Operator	Meaning	Example	Result (for Each Bit Position)
&	Bitwise AND	x & y	1, if 1 in both x and y
|	Bitwise OR	x | y	1, if 1 is in either x or y, but not both
^	Bitwise exclusive OR	x ^ y	1 if 1 in either x or y, but not both
~	Bitwise NOT	~x	1 if 0 in x
^~ or ~^	Bitwise equivalence	x ^~ y or x ~^ y	1, if both 0 or both 1, in other cases, the result is 0
<<	Shift left	x << y	Each bit in x shifted y positions to the left
>>	Shift right	x >> y	Each bit in x shifted y positions to the right

The logical bitwise operators perform boolean bitwise manipulations on the operands, that is, the operator combines a bit in one operand with its corresponding bit in the other operand to calculate one bit for the result. The logical shift operators shift the bits of their operands filling vacated bits with zeros. They should not be used with negative operands. If the bits are shifted beyond the size of the integer, the behavior is undefined.

Conditional Expressions

The conditional expression is the only ternary operator in Verilog-A. The format for the conditional expression is

```
expression-1 ? expression-2 : expression-3
```

The purpose of the conditional expression is to select and evaluate one of two expressions, *expression-2* or *expression-3*, depending on the value of the *expression-1*. If the value of the *expression-1* is zero (0), the value of the conditional expression is *expression-3*; otherwise, it is the value of the *expression-2*:

```
x > y ? x : y // Evaluates the larger of x and y
```

The first operand can be any expression evaluating numeric basic type but the logical expressions or expressions evaluating the integer value are more reliable to use than expressions evaluating real values.

Concatenated Expressions

Concatenated expressions are joining together bits from one or more expressions into a single value using concatenation and replication operators.

The concatenation operator, introduced with brace characters { }, is used to concatenate a comma-separated list of expressions within the braces. For example, the concatenated expression

```
{1'b1, 3'b101}
```

is equivalent to the expression

```
{1'b1, 1'b1, 1'b0, 1'b1}
```

and evaluates to 4'b1101. The value of the concatenated expression

```
{ "hello", " ", "world" }
```

is "hello world".

Unsized basic type values shall not be allowed in concatenations. This is because the size of each operand in the concatenation is needed to calculate the complete size of the concatenation.

Note   Confusion can arise for the Verilog-A users familiar with programming in C because { } is used to describe lists of values for array initialization in the C language, whereas it means something very different (concatenation) in the Verilog-A language.

A replication operator is the only operator that can be applied to concatenated expressions. It is introduced by a concatenation preceded by a non-negative, constant expression, called a replication constant, enclosed together within brace characters. It indicates a joining together of that many copies of the concatenation:

```
{4{w}} // This yields the same value as {w, w, w, w}
{b, {3{a, b}}} // This yields the same value as
              // {b, a, b, a, b, a, b}
result = {4{func(w)}};
```

When a replication expression is evaluated, the operands shall be evaluated exactly once, even if the replication constant is zero (0).

Expression Evaluation Order

The order in which the expressions are evaluated is defined by the operator precedence and associativity. It can be altered using parenthesized expressions and affected by short-circuiting evaluation.

Operator Precedence

In expressions with more than one operator, the precedence of the operators determines the grouping of operands with operators as listed in Table 2-5.

Table 2-5. *Precedence of operators*

Category	Operator	Associativity
Primary	[] ()	Left to right
Unary	! ~ + -	Right to left
Power	**	Left to right
Multiplicative	* / %	Left to right
Additive	+ -	Left to right
Shift	<< >>	Left to right
Relational	< <= > >=	Left to right
Equality	== !=	Left to right
Bitwise	&	Left to right
Bitwise	^ ^~ ~^	Left to right

(*continued*)

Table 2-5. (*continued*)

Category	Operator	Associativity
Bitwise	|	Left to right
Logical	&&	Left to right
Logical	||	Left to right
Conditional	? :	Right to left
Concatenation	{} {{}}	Left to right

For example, the multiplicative arithmetic operators *, /, and % take precedence over additive arithmetic operators + and -. Associativity refers to the order in which the operators having the same precedence are evaluated. If a different grouping is desired, parentheses must be used as a grouping delimiter.

Parenthesized Expressions

Parentheses can be used to alter the default precedence among operators in expressions that contain multiple operators:

```
(a + b) / c // Not the same as a + b / c
```

They are also used as a syntactic aid to mix expressions in ways that would otherwise cause syntactic ambiguities.

Parenthesized expressions could be in principle considered as primary expressions since their values must be evaluated before the expression containing a parenthesized expression is evaluated.

Short-Circuit Evaluation

The logical and conditional expressions in Verilog-A use short-circuit or minimal evaluation. Some of their operand expressions shall not be evaluated if their value is not required to determine the final value of the operation. For example, if in the expression

```
a & (b || c)
```

a is known to be zero, the result of the expression can be determined as zero without evaluating the sub-expression b || c.

All other operators shall not use short-circuit evaluation and all of their operand expressions are always evaluated.

Expression Containers

The expression containers are Verilog-A data structures whose instances are collections of expressions. They store expressions in an organized way that follows specific access rules. Verilog-A supports two types of expression containers: assignment patterns and ranges.

Assignment Patterns

An assignment pattern provides a way to specify a list of expressions of a particular basic type. The list of expressions is grouped as a comma-separated list within the braces { and } prefixed with an apostrophe:

```
'{a, b, c, d}
'{0, 1, 2}
'{1.0, PI/2.0}
'{"first", "middle", "last"};
```

An assignment pattern cannot be used as operand in expressions. Instead, it is used in an assignment-like context. It includes arguments in call operators that are expected to be arrays, initialization of array parameters and variables, and procedural assignments of array variables.

An assignment pattern can nest in another assignment pattern:

```
'{'{0.0,0.1,0.1},'{0.1,0.0,0.1},'{0.1,0.1,0.0}}
```

It allows to annotate a clear correspondence between a collection of expressions and elements in assigned array data objects. A syntax resembling replications can be used in array assignment patterns as well:

```
'{2 {y}} ; // same as '{y, y}
'{2{'{3{y}}}}; // same as '{'{y,y,y},'{y,y,y}}
```

Note   One should be careful not to confuse assignment patterns with a concatenation operator using a pair of braces { } instead of '{ }.

Ranges

When an object in Verilog-A is numerically indexed, the range is used to specify its upper and lower indices.

The range is defined by the syntax

```
[ start-index : end-index ]
```

where *start-index* and *end-index* are constant expressions that shall be evaluated as integers or promoted to integers from real type expressions. The *start-index* and *end-index* can take any positive or negative constant integer value including zero (0):

```
[0 : width-2]
[-7 : 15]
[x/y : -1]
```

The ranges can be either ascending, if *end-index* is greater than *start-index*, or descending if *end-index* is less than *start-index*. It is also possible to have a trivial scalar range if *start-index* is equal to the *end-index*. The use of ascending and descending ranges is entirely up to the user and their conventions.

CHAPTER 3

Net-Discipline Types

In addition to the basic types, Verilog-A also introduces user-defined net-discipline types. The objects of the net-discipline types are nets, an abstraction of connectivity among components of various physical disciplines in Verilog-A models. The net-discipline types encapsulate information on the nature of flow and potential signals, a pair of physical quantities significant for communication and energy exchange among system components. The values of flow and potential signals are used as state variables in system dynamics simulation.

Defining Signal Natures

A nature is a collection of attributes that are shared by a certain class of net signals. Natures should be defined at the top level of the Verilog-A code and they do not nest inside other nature definitions or any other Verilog-A constructs. Natures can be defined as base natures or derived natures that reuse, extend, and modify the base natures. In order to support code portability, the Verilog-A standard provides also a set of predefined nature definitions.

© Slobodan Mijalković 2022
S. Mijalković, *A Practical Guide to Verilog-A*, https://doi.org/10.1007/978-1-4842-6351-8_3

Base Natures

The base natures are defined using the following syntax:

```
nature nature-name ;
    attribute-name = constant-expression ;
  ...
endnature
```

The keyword nature in the header line of the base nature definition is followed by a unique identifier *nature-name* which is used as nature reference. The terminating semicolon (;) after the nature name is optional. A body of the nature definition, between the header line and the keyword endnature, includes a sequence of nature attribute assignment statements. The *attribute-name* could be an identifier or a keyword for standard nature attribute names.

The assignment of three standard attribute names is required for all base nature definitions. The keywords used as attribute names, assigned constant expressions, and short descriptions are given in Table 3-1.

Table 3-1. *Required standard nature attributes*

Attribute Name	Constant Expression	Description
abstol	Real	The maximum negligible value for signals associated with nature
access	Identifier	The name for the signal access function
units	String	A binding between the value of the signal access function and the units for that value

The abstol attribute specifies the maximum negligible value for signals associated with the nature. The constant expression assigned to it shall evaluate a constant real number. The access attribute identifies the unique name of the access function for a potential or flow signal associated with the nature. The constant expression, in that case, shall be an identifier given by name, not as a string. The `units` attribute provides a binding between the value returned by the nature signal access function and the physical unit for that value. It is mostly required for net compatibility checking. Besides, simulators can use `units` attributes to annotate the signals with their physical units.

Here are two examples of the base nature definitions:

```
nature Illuminance
    units       = "Cd";
    access      = LP;
    abstol      = 1e-14;
endnature

nature ChemQ
    units  = "-";
    access = CH;
    abstol = 1e-14;
endnature
```

All other nature attributes are optional and could be assigned in the base as well as in derived natures.

The attribute names, assigned values, and short descriptions for two optional standard nature attributes are given in Table 3-2.

Table 3-2. *Optional built-in nature attributes*

Attribute Name	Constant Expression	Description
ddt_nature	*nature-name*	The name of nature that represents its time derivative
idt_nature	*nature-name*	The name of nature that represents its time integral

The ddt_nature and idt_nature attributes provide a relationship between nature using these attributes in its definition and the natures representing the time derivative and time integral of that nature signal, respectively. These nature attributes are used to reduce the need for specifying numerical tolerances in differential and integral operators ddt() and idt(). The required numerical tolerances can be taken from the ddt_ nature or idt_nature nature abstol attribute values. The value assigned to ddt_nature and idt_nature attributes shall be the nature name given by an identifier, not a string. A nature can reference itself in ddt_nature and idt_nature attribute assignments, which is also the default value for ddt_nature and idt_nature attributes if they are not assigned.

Here are examples of nature definitions including ddt_nature and idt_nature attribute assignments:

```
nature Voltage;
    units = "V";
    access = V;
    idt_nature = Flux;
    abstol = 1e-6;
endnature

nature Flux;
    units = "Wb";
    access = Phi;
    ddt_nature = Voltage;
    abstol = 1e-9;
endnature
```

In addition to the required and optional standard nature attributes, a nature definition can also assign optional user-defined attribute names. Typical examples include the maximum and minimum signal values or other numerical range signal properties:

```
nature my_current;
    units = "A";
    access = I;
    abstol = 1u;
    reltol = 1m; // user-defined attribute
endnature
```

A user-defined attribute can be assigned in the same manner as the standard attributes but using an identifier as the attribute name. The attribute name shall be unique in the nature being defined and the assigned values shall be constant.

Derived Natures

A nature can be derived from a parent nature, which is an already defined base nature or other derived nature. The derived nature inherits all the attributes of the parent nature.

A derived nature is defined using the extended syntax for the nature definition header line:

```
nature nature-name :  parent-nature ;
```

where the derived and parent nature names are separated by a colon (:) character.

A derived nature can assign additional attributes or override attribute values of the parent nature:

```
nature new_current : my_current;
    abstol = 1m; // modified for this nature
    maxval = 10.0; // new attribute for this nature
endnature
```

It is illegal for a derived nature to assign or change the access and units attributes. It is possible to modify the parent's values of ddt_nature and idt_nature attributes if the derived nature is related (share the same base nature) to the nature that the parent nature uses for its ddt_nature and idt_nature attributes.

Without any new attribute assignments and attribute overrides:

```
nature net_current : new_current; // An alias
endnature
```

the derived nature is identical to the parent nature and essentially represents an alias for the parent nature name.

Predefined Natures

The names and attribute assignments of the Verilog-A predefined standard natures are summarized in Table 3-3.

Table 3-3. Predefined standard natures

Nature Name	Units	Access	Abstol	idt_nature	ddt_nature
Current	"A"	I	1e-12	Charge	-
Charge	"coul"	Q	1e-14		Current
Voltage	"V"	V	1e-6	Flux	-
Flux	"Wb"	Phi	1e-9	-	Voltage
Magneto_Motive_Force	"A*turn"	MMF	1e-12	-	-
Temperature	"K"	Temp	1e-4	-	-
Power	"W"	Pwr	1e-9	-	-
Position	"m"	Pos	1e-6	-	Velocity
Velocity	"m/s"	Vel	1e-6	Position	Acceleration
Acceleration	"m/s^2"	Acc	1e-6	Velocity	Impulse
Impulse	"m/s^3"	Imp	1e-6	Acceleration	-
Force	"N"	F	1e-6	-	-
Angle	"rads/s^2"	Alpha	1e-6	-	Angular_ Velocity

(continued)

Table 3-3. (*continued*)

Nature Name	Units	Access	Abstol	idt_nature	ddt_nature
Angular_Velocity	"rads/s"	Omega	1e-6	Angle	Angular-Acceleration
Angular_Acceleration	"rads/s^2"	Alpha	1e-6	Angular_Velocity	-
Angular_Force	"Nm"	Tau	1e-6	-	-

The predefined standard natures can be accessed in discipline definitions by including the standard `disciplines.vams` file as explained in Chapter 20.

Defining Net-Discipline Types

The net-discipline types are defined using the syntax

```
discipline discipline-name ;
    discipline-statement
    ...
enddiscipline
```

The keyword `discipline` in the header line of the discipline definition is followed by a unique identifier *discipline-name* which is used as a net-discipline type name in net declarations. The use of the semicolon (;) in the discipline definition header line is optional. The discipline shall be defined at the top level of the Verilog-A code and they do not nest inside other discipline definitions or any other Verilog-A constructs.

A body of the discipline definition, between the header line and the keyword `enddiscipline`, contains a sequence of nature binding, domain binding, and nature override discipline statements.

Nature Binding Statements

The nature binding statements are used to associate the discipline potential and flow signal quantities to the corresponding natures:

```
potential  nature-name ;
flow  nature-name ;
```

The keywords `potential` and `flow` are used for the potential and flow binding, respectively.

Disciplines having both potential and flow nature bindings are known as conservative disciplines:

```
discipline electrical;
    potential Voltage;
    flow Current;
enddiscipline
```

Conservative disciplines shall not have the same nature specified for both the potential and the flow.

Disciplines defined with a single potential or flow nature binding statement are signal-flow disciplines:

```
discipline optical_sf
    potential Illuminance;
enddiscipline
```

```
discipline chemical_sf
    potential ChemQ;
enddiscipline
```

In principle, it is possible to define a discipline with no nature bindings. These are known as natureless or empty disciplines:

```
discipline natureless;
enddiscipline
```

The nets declared with empty disciplines can be used in structural descriptions but not in signal access functions since the nature of signals is not known. Usage of empty disciplines is highly discouraged. They are mainly provided for backward compatibility with previous versions of the Verilog-A standards.

Domain Binding Statements

The discipline definition syntax allows also the specification of the nature signal domain using one of the domain binding statements:

```
domain discrete;
domain continuous;
```

The domain binding statements are optional. The default value for a domain is `continuous`.

Since analog signals are always represented in continuous time, a Verilog-A compiler shall silently ignore any definition of a discipline with a `discrete` domain binding.

Nature Override Statements

A discipline can override the value of the predefined attributes in the bound natures using attribute override statements:

```
potential . attribute-name = constant-expression ;
flow . attribute-name = constant-expression ;
```

The attribute names are accessed using the keyword `potential` or `flow`, followed by the hierarchical punctuator (`.`), and an attribute name.

In the following example, the discipline `enode` overrides the value of the `abstol` and `maxval` attributes in `new_current` nature:

```
discipline enode;
    potential Voltage;
    flow new_current;
    flow.abstol = 10u;
    flow.maxval = 1K;
enddiscipline
```

The restrictions imposed on the attribute overrides in derived natures hold also for nature override statements in discipline definitions.

Deriving Natures from Disciplines

A nature can be also derived from the natures bound to the potential or flow in a discipline. It can be achieved using one of the following nature definition headers:

```
nature derived-nature-name : discipline-name . potential ;
nature derived-nature-name : discipline-name . flow ;
```

where the parent nature name is replaced by the discipline name followed by the hierarchical punctuator (.) and the keyword flow or potential. The derived nature in this way inherits all the attributes of the nature bound to the potential or the flow of the discipline. If the nature binding to the potential or the flow of a discipline changes, the new nature shall automatically inherit the attributes of the changing nature.

A nature derived from the flow or potential of a discipline can declare additional attributes or override values of the attributes already declared as any other derived nature.

```
nature enode_curr : enode.flow;
    reltol = 1u; // modified for this nature
    minval = 1p; // new attribute for this nature
endnature
```

In the preceding example, the nature enode_curr is derived from the natures bound to flow in the discipline enode.

Discipline Compatibility

Certain operations can be done on nets only if the two (or more) nets are compatible. For example, if a signal access function has two nets as arguments, they must be compatible. It shall be an error to connect two nets with incompatible disciplines.

The following rules shall apply to determine discipline compatibility:

- A discipline is compatible with itself.

- Disciplines with incompatible potential natures are incompatible.

- Disciplines with incompatible flow natures are incompatible.

The following rules shall apply to determine nature compatibility:

- A nature is compatible with itself.

- A potential or flow nature is compatible with a nonexistent potential or flow nature binding.

- A derived nature is compatible with its base nature.

- Two natures are compatible if they are derived from the same base nature.

- Two natures are compatible if they have the same value for the units attribute.

The following examples illustrate these rules:

```
discipline electrical;
    potential Voltage;
    flow Current;
endnature

discipline highvolt;
    potential highvoltage;
    flow Current;
endnature

discipline sig_flow_v;
    potential Voltage;
enddiscipline
```

```
nature Voltage;
    access = V;
    units = "V";
    abstol = 1u;
endnature

nature highvoltage : Voltage;
    abstol = 1;
endnature
```

The Voltage and highvoltage natures are compatible because highvoltage nature is derived from Voltage nature. Similarly, electrical and highvolt disciplines are compatible because the natures for both potential and flow exist and are derived from the same base natures. The disciplines electrical and sig_flow_v are compatible because the nature for potential is the same for both disciplines and the nature for flow does not exist in sig_flow_v.

When a net is connected to other nets with compatible disciplines, the net shall be treated as having a potential abstol with a value equal to the smallest abstol of all the potential natures of all the disciplines with which it is connected. The net shall be treated as having a flow abstol with a value equal to the smallest abstol of all the flow natures, if any, of all the disciplines with which it is connected.

Predefined Disciplines

Together with the predefined standard nature definitions given in Table 3-3, Verilog-A also provides a set of predefined discipline definitions which are summarized in Table 3-4.

Table 3-4. *Predefined standard disciplines*

Discipline	Potential Nature	Flow Nature
electrical	Voltage	Current
voltage	Voltage	-
current	-	Current
magnetic	Magneto_Motive_Force	Flux
thermal	Temperature	Power
kinematic	Position	Force
kinematic_v	Velocity	Force
rotational	Angle	Angular_Force
rotational_omega	Angular_Velocity	Angular_Force

The predefined standard disciplines can be used for net declaration in Verilog-A code by including the standard `disciplines.vams` file using the include compiler directive as explained in Chapter 20.

Net Declarations

Nets are declared as objects of the net-discipline types. Nets can be declared as scalar or vector nets.

Scalar Nets

The scalar nets are declared using a declaration statement:

```
discipline-name net-name, ... ;
```

Here, *discipline-name* is the identifier of an already defined discipline. It is followed by a comma-separated list of net identifiers or hierarchical names:

```
kinematic ki_gnd, tmass;
electrical el_gnd, tetop, tebot, tesens, tesensa,
           ttrig, tinv;
chemical_sf c_NaN3, c_Na, c_N2, c_KNO3, c_K2O,
            c_Na2O, c_SiO2, c_K2Na2SiO4;
thermal tjsrc, tjn, tjp, tjld, tjpd, top.foo.dt;
optical_sf light_out, light_prop;
```

In the preceding examples, `kinematic`, `electrical`, and `thermal` disciplines are predefined conservative disciplines, while `optical_sf` and `chemical_sf` are user-defined signal-flow disciplines.

Vector Nets

Nets can be also declared as vectors specifying the vector range after the discipline name in the declaration statement:

```
net-discipline-type-name range net-name, ... ;
```

The range specifier is associated with the net-discipline type declaration, not the *net-name* identifier, and it is common for all nets in the declaration comma-separated list.

```
electrical [0:width-1] in;
voltage [5:0] n2, n3;
```

Ground Nets

The potential of a net is always defined with respect to a global reference net, or ground net. Scalar and vector nets can be declared to be the global reference nets using the ground declaration statement:

```
ground net-name, ... ;
ground range net-name, ... ;
```

where *net-name* should be previously declared with its net-discipline:

```
electrical gnd;
thermal [0:1] dt;
...
ground gnd;
ground [0:1] dt;
```

The vector ranges in discipline and ground declaration shall be of the same size.

The Verilog-A standard supports also an alternative and less verbose syntax for ground declarations:

```
ground discipline-name net-name, ... ;
ground discipline-name range net-name, ... ;
```

allowing to specify ground net-discipline in the ground declaration statements:

```
ground electrical gnd;
ground thermal [0:1] dt;
```

It avoids repeating port names and ranges in separate net-discipline and ground declarations.

Net Initialization

Nets are allowed to have initializers as a part of their declarations. The net initialization sets the values for the potential signal in declared nets.

The initialization is introduced into net declarations by replacing the *net-name* identifiers or hierarchical names with assignments:

```
discipline-name net-name=initializer, ... ;
discipline-name range net-name=initializer, ... ;
```

For scalar nets, the initializer shall be a real type constant expression:

```
electrical a = 5.0;
mechanical top.foo.w = 250.0;
```

For vector nets, an assignment pattern with a list of real type constant expression is used as an initializer.

```
electrical [0:4] pins = '{2.3,4.5, ,6.0};
```

A missing value in the assignment pattern list indicates that no initial value is being specified for this element of the vector net.

If different nets in contact have conflicting initializers, then initializers on hierarchical net declarations win. If there are multiple hierarchical declarations, then the declaration on the highest level wins. If there are multiple hierarchical declarations on the highest level, then it is a race condition for which the initializer wins. If the multiple conflicting initializers are not hierarchical, then it is also a race condition for which the initializer wins.

Accessing Net Attributes

Net-discipline types encapsulate the values of potential and flow signal intensities and corresponding nature attribute values. The values of attributes attached to the potential or flow natures of the declared net can be accessed using hierarchical names with the syntax:

net-name . potential . *attribute-name*
net-name . flow . *attribute-name*

For example, the hierarchical name

n1.flow.maxval

can be used in expressions as a value of the user-defined attribute maxval if the net n1 is declared as enode net-discipline type.

The intensity of net potential and flow signals can be accessed only indirectly using signal access functions described in Chapter 8.

CHAPTER 4

Modules and Ports

Modules are fundamental building blocks for structural and behavioral system description in the Verilog-A language. Ports provide module connectivity and allow communication between a module and its environment. When working on large designs, it is a common practice to decompose a system into a set of interconnected modules representing system components. Verilog-A supports a hierarchical system design by allowing modules to be instantiated within other modules. Higher-level modules create instances of lower-level modules and communicate with them through input, output, and bidirectional ports.

Defining Module Connectivity

Modules are basically defined using the syntax:

```
module module-name ( module-connectivity ) ;
        // Module items
    ...
endmodule
```

The keyword module in the module header line, ending with a semicolon (;), is followed by a unique identifier *module-name* and a specification of the module connectivity in the parentheses. The top-level modules, without external connectivity, use header lines without, or with empty, parentheses. The module headers can be also used to declare module parameters, as it is described in the next chapter.

S. Mijalković, *A Practical Guide to Verilog-A*, https://doi.org/10.1007/978-1-4842-6351-8_4

53

Note   The keyword `macromodule` could be used interchangeably with the keyword `module` in the module header line. A compiler implementation may choose to treat module definitions beginning with the `macromodule` keyword differently, but in principle, the `macromodule` is just a synonym for a `module`.

Between the header line and the keyword `endmodule` is a module body containing a sequence of module items that define a module. Modules are defined at the top level of the Verilog-A code and they do not nest, that is, one module definition does not contain the text of another module definition. Each module definition stands alone.

Most of the Verilog-A language constructs are module items. The only exceptions are the nature and discipline definitions described in Chapter 3 and paramset definitions that will be introduced in Chapter 6. The other Verilog-A constructs must be defined and used only within the scope of a module body. But before we address Verilog-A module items in the following chapters, it is essential to first define module connectivity by declaring port directions and types.

Declaring Port Directions

Ports provide connectivity to a module by sending and receiving signals from the outside world. The ports are basically declared with the direction of the signal flow through a port. Verilog-A supports two syntax forms for port declaration.

In the first syntax form, the module ports are specified in a module header and declared in a module body:

```
module module-name ( port-name, ... );
port-declaration ; ...
    // Other module items
    ...
endmodule
```

In this case, the parentheses in the module header contain an ordered list of comma-separated identifiers specifying port names. A compiler implementation can limit the maximum number of module ports, but it should allow at least 256 ports. The order used in defining a list of port names can be significant when instantiating the module.

The actual port declarations are introduced as statements in the module body together with other module items. Port can be declared as scalar or vector ports. The syntax for scalar *port-declaration* is

```
direction port-name,  ...
```

The *direction* specifier can be either input or output keyword for unidirectional or inout keyword for bidirectional port declaration. The direction specifier is followed by a comma-separated list of port names. All ports listed in the module header should have a direction declaration in a module body.

Here are examples of bidirectional and unidirectional scalar port declarations in modules representing a MOS transistor, a light-emitting diode (LED), and a photodiode:

```
module mosekv (d, g, s, b, dt);
    inout d, g, s, b, dt;
    ...
endmodule
```

55

```
module led (anode, cathode, out_light);
   inout anode, cathode;
   output out_light;
   ...
endmodule
```

```
module photodiode (in_light, anode, cathode);
   input in_light,
   inout anode, cathode;
   ...
endmodule
```

The dots in the module body indicate that the modules contain also other items which are not relevant for the port declaration.

The vector ports are declared similar to vector nets:

```
direction range port-name,  ...
```

introducing a range specifier after the direction specifier. Here is an example of vector port declaration in a module representing a neural network unit:

```
module perceptron (in, out);
   input  [10:0] in;
   output out;
   ...
endmodule
```

Note that the vector port names declared in the module body are listed in the module header without range specifications.

Verilog-A supports also an alternative syntax for a port declaration that is similar to the ANSI C style of function argument declaration:

```
module module-name ( port-declaration, ... );
    // Other module items
    ...
endmodule
```

In this syntax form, the list of port declarations is specified in the module header instead of the module body. Note that the port declarations in module headers do not end with a statement terminator (;) as the port declaration statements in the module body. Ports declared in the module header shall not be redeclared within the body of the module. It also is not allowed to mix module body and header port declarations.

Using this syntax form, we can redefine the port declarations in mosekv and led, photodiode, and perceptron module headers as

```
module mosekv (inout d, g, s, b,
               inout dt);

module led (inout anode, catode,
            output out_light);

module photodiode (input in_light,
                   inout anode, catode);

module perceptron (inout [10:0] in,
                   output out);
```

The port declaration in the module header is more concise and avoids repeating port names in the module header and body.

Declaring Port Types

Ports are essentially nets and therefore each declared port needs also a net-discipline declaration in order to be used in the behavioral Verilog-A system description. If the port type is not declared, the port can only be used in structural descriptions of system connectivity.

The port types can be declared in a module body using the net declaration statements described in Chapter 3:

```
module mosekv (d, g, s, b, dt);
    inout d, g, s, b, dt;

    electrical d, g, s, b;
    thermal dt;
    ...
endmodule

module led (anode, cathode, out_light);

    inout anode, catode;
    output out_light;

    electrical anode, cathode;
    optical_sf olight;
    ...
endmodule

module photodiode (in_light, anode, cathode);
    input ilight,
    inout anode, cathode;

    optical_sf in_light;
    electrical anode, cathode;
    ...
endmodule

module perceptron (in, out);
    input [10:0] in;
    output out;
```

```
   voltage out;
   voltage [10:0] in;
   ...
endmodule
```

An important difference is that it is not allowed to initialize the port potential signal values:

```
thermal dt = 27.0; // illegal initialization
```

The ranges in the vector port direction and net-discipline declarations should be identical:

```
voltage [0:10] in; // wrong range, should be [10:0]
```

Unidirectional ports, with input and output directions, may only be declared as signal-flow net-discipline types, and bidirectional ports, with inout direction, as conservative net-discipline types.

Verilog-A supports also an alternative and less verbose syntax for direction and net-discipline declaration of scalar and vector ports:

```
direction net-discipline  port-name,  ... ;
direction net-discipline [  index1 : index2 ]  port-
name,  ... ;
```

Basically, it allows declaring a port type within the port declaration. It can be used in the port declaration statements in a module body:

```
inout electrical anode, cathode;
inout voltage [10:0] in;
```

but most effectively it is used for port declaration in the module headers:

```
module mosekv (inout electrical d, g, s, b,
               inout thermal dt);
```

```
module laserdiode (inout electrical anode, catode,
                   output optical_sf out_light);

module photodiode (input optical_sf in_light,
                   inout elecrical anode, catode);

module perceptron (inout voltage [10:0] in,
                   output voltage out);
```

This syntax enhancement reduces the amount of code required to declare all the information on port connectivity. It also prevents syntax errors due to incompatible vector port ranges.

Connecting Modules by Instantiation

The only way to connect modules is to instantiate them in higher-level modules. A hierarchy of interconnected modules in Verilog-A is created by recursive module instantiations.

The module instantiation statement creates one or more named instances of a module. The basic syntax of the module instantiating statements is

module-name   module-instance, ...   ;

where a *module-name* identifier must match exactly the name of the previously declared module or one declared later. The comma-separated list of module instances follows the module name. The module instantiation statement can also include a list of parameter assignments after the module name, as discussed in the next chapter.

The *module-instance* in module instantiation statements is specified as

module-instance-name   (port-connection, ...)

introducing a *module-instance-name* identifier and a comma-separated list of port connections in the parentheses. A list of port connections in parentheses is optional because it is possible to instantiate also top modules. The parentheses, however, are always required.

The instantiations of modules can contain a range specification:

```
module-instance-name  range ( port-connection, ... )
```

which allows an array of instances to be created. These instances shall have the same name and differ from each other only by the index in the range specifier. One instance identifier shall be associated with only one range to declare an array of instances.

The *port-connection* in the module instance specification provides a mapping of a port in module definition and instance. There are two techniques to define *port-connection*, explicit and positional. The explicit and positional port mappings shall not be mixed in the same module instantiation. The connections to the ports of a particular module instance shall be all explicit or all positional.

Explicit Port Mapping

The explicit way to connect module ports consists of linking the two names for each side of the connection using the syntax:

```
. module-port-name ( instance-mapping )
```

where *module-port-name*, preceded with a period (.), shall be the port name specified in the module definition. The instance port mapping is enclosed within parentheses. For scalar ports, the *instance-mapping* shall be a simple net identifier or a scalar member of a vector net or port declared within the module. For vector ports, it could be a subrange of a vector net or port declared within the module, or a vector net formed as a result of the concatenation operator.

An unconnected port can be indicated by omitting it in the list of port connections or using empty parentheses in port mapping:

. *module-port-name*( )

The parentheses, however, are always required. In that way, the instantiating module can document the existence of the port without connecting it to anything. The port connections can be listed in any order since the details of the connection (module port to instance port name) are explicit.

The following examples illustrate the module instantiation with explicit port mapping:

```
module cmos_invertor (in, out, dt, vdd, vss);

    inout in, out, dt, vdd;
    electrical in, out, vdd, vss;
    thermal dt;

    mosekv mp (.g(in),
               .d(out),
               .s(vdd),
               .dt(dt),
               .b(vdd));

    mosekv mn (.dt(dt),
               .g(in),
               .b(vss),
               .s(vss),
               .d(out));
endmodule

module opto_coupler (aled, kled, aphd, kphd)
    optical_sf ir_beam;
    electrical aled, kled, aphd, kphd;
```

```
    led dio (.cat(kled),
            .ano(aled),
            .out_light(ir_beam));

    photodiode phd (.ano(aphd),
                   .in_light(ir_beam),
                   .cat(kphd));
endmodule

module nn_test (input voltage [10:0] a,
               input voltage [5:0] b
               output voltage [0:1] c);

    perceptron pct1 (.in(a),
                    .out(c[0]));
    perceptron pct2 (.in('{a[4:0], b}),
                    .out(c[1]));
endmodule
```

It is recommended to code each port connection in a separate line as much easier to debug and resolve compilation errors.

Positional Port Mapping

The other way to connect the ports in an instantiated module with the ports in a module definition is via an ordered list, that is, the ports listed for the module instance shall be in the same order as the ports listed in the module definition. The cmos_invertor, opto_coupler, and nn_test modules can be redefined using the positional port mapping as

```
module cmos_invertor (in, out, dt, vdd, vss);

    inout in, out, dt, vdd;
    electrical in, out, vdd, vss;
```

```
   mosekv mp (out, in, vdd, vdd, dt);
   mosekv mn (out, in, vss, vss, dt);
endmodule

module opto_coupler (aled, kled, aphd, kphd)
   optical_sf ir_beam;
   electrical aled, kled, aphd, kphd;

   led dio (aled, kled, ir_beam);
   photodiode phd (ir_beam, aphd, kphd);
endmodule

module nn_test (input voltage [10:0] a,
                input voltage [5:0] b
                output voltage [0:1] c);

   perceptron pct1 (a, c[0]);
   perceptron pct2 ('{a[4:0], b}, c[1]);
endmodule
```

This approach requires less text to describe the connection but can also easily lead to misconnections due to inadvertent mistakes in the port order. The list of module connections shall be provided only for modules defined with ports.

A blank port connection shall represent the situation where the port is not to be connected.

Top-Level Instantiation and $root

The hierarchy of instantiated modules can be viewed as a tree structure, where each module instance defines a new branch of the hierarchy. The modules that are included in the Verilog-A source text but do not appear in any module instantiation statement are top-level modules. In the following example, the module airbag is a top module of the airbag system:

```
module airbag;

    kinematic mass, ki_gnd;
    electrical esens;
    voltage etrig, chtrig;
    ground ki_gnd;

    impact_force fsrc  (mass, ki_gnd);
    sensor        msens (mass, esens);
    comparator    scomp (esens, etrig);
    trigger              chtrg (etrig, chtrig)
    chemsys       chsys (chtrig);

endmodule
```

A Verilog-A design shall contain at least one top-level module. A top-level module is implicitly instantiated once, and its instance name is the same as the module name. Such an instance is called a top-level instance.

The hierarchy of instantiated modules defines a hierarchical name for every declared identifier in the module definitions. Any named object can be referenced uniquely by its hierarchical name. Hierarchical names consist of module instance names separated by periods (.), where an instance name can be also an element of the instantiated module array. The system name $root refers to the top of the instantiated design:

```
$root.airbag.mass
$root.airbag.msens.etop
```

If $root is not specified, a hierarchical path could be ambiguous. For example, A.B.C can mean the local A.B.C or the top-level A.B.C, assuming there is an instance A that contains an instance B at both the top level and in the current module. The ambiguity is resolved by giving priority to the local scope and thereby preventing access to the top-level path. $root allows explicit access to the top level in those cases in which the name of the top-level module is insufficient to uniquely identify the path.

Implicit Nets

Nets appearing in the connection lists of a module instantiation need not be declared in the instantiating module. Their net-discipline type will be determined by discipline resolution.

In the module th_network defined as follows, it is not necessary to declare the net-discipline type of dt1 and dt2. It will be implicitly defined by the resolution of disciplines in lower-level modules connected via dt1 and dt2:

```
module th_network (dtin, dtout);

    inout dtin, dtout;
    thermal dtin, dtout tref;
    ground tref

    // dt1 and dt2 are implicit nets, not declared
    resth  rth1  (.p(dtin),
                  .m(dt1));
    capth  cth1  (.p(in),
                  .m(tref));
    resth  rth2  (.p(dt1),
                  .m(dt2));
    capth  cth2  (.p(tin),
                  .m(tref));
    resth  rth3  (.p(dt2),
                  .t(dtout));
endmodule
```

Ports can be used in structural descriptions also without net declarations. If the net-discipline type of a port is not declared, or declared with natureless disciplines, the port can only be used in a structural description. It can be passed to instances of modules, but cannot be accessed in behavioral descriptions. The use of undeclared net and ports is not recommended practice.

Instantiation of SPICE Primitives

If a simulator supports SPICE compatibility, it is expected to provide the basic set of SPICE primitives for instantiation in Verilog-A modules. The instantiation of SPICE primitives can be mixed with module instantiation.

For example, the module sensor defined as follows is instantiating SPICE primitive vsine representing sinusoidal voltage sources:

```
module sensor(inout kinematic mass,
              inout electrical esens);

    electrical el_gnd, etop, ebot;
    ground el_gnd;

    accel acm (.mass(mass),
               .tmref(kin_gnd),
               .etop(etop),
               .emid(esens),
               .ebot(ebot));

    vsine vsrct (etop, el_gnd);
    vsine vsrcb (ebot, el_gnd);

endmodule
```

The SPICE primitives can be only instantiated with positional port mapping. The default discipline of the ports for these primitives shall be electrical and their direction shall be inout.

The required names for SPICE primitives and ports are shown in Appendix in Table A-1. However, the names of the built-in SPICE primitives and their ports can differ from simulator to simulator.

CHAPTER 5

Parameters

Verilog-A provides parameters as module runtime basic type constants. Parameters allow a module to be reused with a different specification and to customize a module's structural and behavioral descriptions for different functionalities. The module instantiation and hierarchical parameter override allow changing values of parameters at the elaboration time to have values that are different from those specified in the parameter declarations. Verilog-A also provides system parameters that are implicitly declared for every module.

Parameter Declarations

A module is parameterized by introducing one or more parameter declarations into the module definition. Parameters are declared either in a module body, as statements terminated by a semicolon (;), or in a module header, as a list of comma-separated parameter declarations, grouped in parentheses preceded by a (#) punctuator:

```
module module-name #( parameter-declaration, ... )
                ( list-of-ports-or-port-declarations );
      parameter-declaration ; ...
        // Other module items
endmodule
```

© Slobodan Mijalković 2022
S. Mijalković, *A Practical Guide to Verilog-A*, https://doi.org/10.1007/978-1-4842-6351-8_5

Parameter declaration statements could be positioned anywhere within a module body. However, Verilog-A requires parameters to be declared before being used in other module items. Note that parameter declarations in a module header precede the list of ports or port declarations. It allows the parameterization of vector port ranges declared in the module headers.

A parameter is declared as a runtime constant of the basic type using a syntax:

```
parameter basic-type parameter-assignment, ...
```

where the keyword `parameter` is followed by the basic type specifier, which shall be a `real`, `integer`, or `string` keyword, and a comma-separated list of parameter assignments.

Parameter assignments specify parameters as simple or array quantities and assign them default values. Optionally, parameter assignment can specify ranges of permissible parameter values. It is possible to declare an alternate name or alias for parameters and to declare parameters as all-time constants or local parameters.

Simple Parameters

The syntax for the specification and default value assignment of a simple parameter is

```
parameter-name =  constant-expression
```

where *parameter-name* is an identifier, and the constant expression after the equal sign (=) has a compatible basic type as the parameter type:

```
parameter integer size = 16;
parameter real slew_rate = 1e-3;
parameter string transistortype = "NMOS"
```

The constant expression in the parameter default value assignments can also use values of the previously assigned parameter default values:

```
parameter real
   gate_width = 0.3e-6,
   gate_length = 4.0e-6,
   gate_area = gate_length * gate_width;
```

If the type of the parameter is specified as integer or real, and the value assigned to the parameter conflicts with the type of the parameter, the value is converted to the type of the parameter:

```
parameter real size = 10; // size is coerced to 10.0.
```

No conversion shall be applied for strings. It shall be an error to assign a numeric value to a parameter declared as a string or to assign a string value to a real parameter.

Array Parameters

The array parameters are declared by adding one or more range specifiers after the parameter name:

```
parameter-name   range ... =   constant-assignment-pattern
```

and using a constant assignment pattern to define the array parameter default values. It is the assignment pattern containing only constant basic type numbers and identifiers of previously declared parameters:

```
parameter real poles[0:3]='{ 1.0,3.198,4.554,2.00 };
parameter real c[0:2][0:2] =
   '{'{0.0,0.2,0.2},'{0.2,0.0,0.2},'{0.2,0.2,0.0}};
```

Since the array range in the parameter array declaration may depend on previously declared parameters, the array size may be changed by overriding the appropriate parameters. If the array size is changed, the parameter array shall be assigned an array of the new size from the same module as the parameter assignment that changed the parameter array size.

Permissible Value Ranges

A parameter assignment can contain optional specifications of the permissible ranges of the parameter values. More than one value range can be specified for the inclusion or exclusion of parameter permissible values. The value of a parameter is checked against the specified permissible value range. It shall be an error only if the value of the parameter is out of range during simulation.

Note   Parameter range checking applies to the value of the parameter for the instance and not against the default values specified in the parameter declaration.

The following constructs can be used for the specification of permissible parameter values:

```
from start-bracket min-value : max-value end-bracket
exclude start-bracket min-value : max-value end-bracket
exclude constant-expression
```

where *start-bracket* is either (or [, while *end-bracket* is either) or]. Square brackets, [and], indicate the inclusion of the endpoints in the valid range. Round brackets or parentheses, (and), indicate the exclusion of the endpoints from the valid range. It is possible to include one endpoint and not the other using [ ) and ( ]. The first expression in the range shall be numerically smaller than the second expression in the range:

```
parameter real neg_bias = -15.0 from [-50:0);
parameter integer pos_bias = 15.0 from (0:50);
parameter real gain = 1 from [1:1000];
```

Here, the parameter neg_bias is only allowed to acquire values within the range of -50 <= neg_bias < 0. Similarly, the parameter pos_bias is only allowed to acquire values within the range of 0 < pos_bias < 50. And, the parameter gain is allowed to acquire values within the range of 1 <= gain <= 1000.

The keyword inf can be used to indicate infinity. To specify that the parameter has no bound on one end, the endpoint is given to either be -inf, if it is the left endpoint, or inf if it is on the right:

```
parameter real val1 = 0.0 from (-inf:0];
parameter real val2 = 0.0 from [0:inf);
```

The exclude keyword is used to define exclusions of the permissible ranges of parameter values. For example, the permissible values of the parameter neg_bias can be also specified as

```
parameter real neg_bias = -15.0
                exclude (-inf:-50) exclude [0:inf);
```

A single value can be excluded from the valid values for a parameter:

```
parameter integer dir = 1 from [-1:1] exclude 0;
```

When used in array parameter declarations:

```
parameter real poles[0:3] =
        '{ 1.0, 3.198, 4.554, 2.00 } from [0:inf);
```

the same permissible value ranges apply to each element of the parameter array.

Valid values of string parameters are indicated using assignment patterns with lists of valid string values as shown in the parameter declarations for the mosekv module:

```
module mosekv (d, g, s, b, dt);
    inout d, g, s, b, dt;

    electrical d, g, s, b;
    thermal dt;

    parameter string TYPE = "NMOS"
                            from '{ "NMOS", "PMOS" };
    parameter real WEFF  = 1.0u from (0.0:inf);
    parameter real LEFF  = 0.15u from (0.0:inf);
    parameter real VTO   = 0.4;
    parameter real TCV   = 1.5m;
    parameter real PHI   = 0.97;
    parameter real GAMMA = 0.7 from [0.0:inf);
    parameter real KP    = 150.0u;
    parameter real THETA = 50.0m;
    parameter real BEX   = -1.5;

    ...
endmodule
```

The string parameter TYPE is permitted to have either "NMOS" or "PMOS" value. In the example:

```
parameter string filename = "output.dat"
                            exclude '{ "" };
```

the parameter filename cannot be given as an empty string.

Parameter Aliases

Verilog-A allows defining parameter aliases as alternative parameter names. Multiple aliases can point to the same parameter. The parameter aliases shall not conflict with other parameter names. Parameter aliases allow using different names for the same parameter when overriding module parameter values. The other module items shall reference the parameter only by its original name, not the alias.

The syntax of alias parameter declaration is

```
aliasparam alias-name = parameter-name ;
```

where the identifier *alias-name* is the alternative name for the *parameter-name*:

```
parameter real BETA0 = 0.0 from [0:inf);
aliasparam BETAO = BETA0;
```

Here, the parameter alias allows to access parameter BETA0 in parameter overrides also as BETAO, with the letter "O" in place of the number "0". The type of an alias shall be determined by the original parameter, as is its range of permissible values if specified. When overriding parameters, it shall be an error to specify an override for a parameter using both its original name and alias (or more aliases), regardless of how the override is done (by name or using the defparam statement).

Local Parameters

Verilog-A provides also "true" constants, called local parameters, which cannot be directly redefined by a parameter override at the elaboration time. The declaration of local parameters uses the same syntax as the declaration of regular parameters and only replaces the keyword parameter with the keyword `localparam`:

```
localparam real ttransit = 1/freq;
localparam real tox = 3e-8;
localparam Csec = Cap/N, Rsec = Res/N;
```

The use of local parameters in a module is identical to parameters except that they cannot be directly redefined from outside the module. However, a local parameter can be still assigned the default value using an expression involving regular parameters and can therefore be indirectly redefined.

Overriding Parameters

Parameters can be modified at elaboration time to have values that are different from those specified in the declaration assignments. It can be done by the instance or hierarchical parameter override.

Instance Parameter Override

When one module instantiates another module, it can alter the values of any parameters declared within the instantiated module. It is achieved by inserting a list of comma-separated parameter override assignments in the parentheses preceded by the punctuator (#) after the module name identifier and before the list of module instances:

module-name #(*parameter-override, ...) module-instance, ... ;*

It is not possible to override parameter aliases. The instance parameter override construct comes in two forms, by name or by ordered list.

Parameter Override by Name

The instance parameter override by name explicitly associates parameter names with the overriding parameter values using the following syntax for *parameter-override*:

. *parameter-name* (`constant-expression`)

The *parameter-name* shall be the same name specified in the parameter declaration of the instantiated module. It is not necessary to assign values to all the parameters within a module when using this method. Only those parameters which are assigned new values need to be specified. Once a parameter is assigned a new value, there shall not be another assignment to this parameter name. The use of *constant-expression* is optional:

. *parameter-name* ( )

It allows the instantiating module to document the existence of a parameter without assigning anything value to it. The parentheses are required, and in this case, the parameter retains its default value. An array assigned to an instance of a module to override the default value of an array parameter shall be of the exact size of the parameter array, as determined by its declaration.

In the following example of instantiating a voltage-controlled oscillator, the parameters are overridden on a named-association basis:

```
module cmos_invertor (in, out, dt, vdd, vss);

    inout in, out, dt, vdd;
    electrical in, out, vdd, vss;
    thermal dt;
```

```
parameter real WP = 60.0u;
parameter real WN = 30.0u;
parameter real LP = 0.15u;
parameter real LN = 0.15u;

mosekv #(.TYPE("PMOS"),
         .WEFF(WP),
         .LEFF(LP),
         .VTO(-0.4),
         .TCV(-1.5e-3))
    mp (.g(in),
        .d(out),
        .s(vdd),
        .dt(dt),
        .b(vdd));

mosekv #(.TYPE("NMOS"),
         .WEFF(WN),
         .LEFF(LN),
         .VTO(0.4),
         .TCV(1.5e-3))

    mn (.dt(dt),
        .g(in),
        .b(vss),
        .s(vss),
        .d(out));
endmodule
```

Parameter Override by Order

The instance parameter override by order allows parameter values to be overridden during module instantiation in the order of their declaration within the module. In that case, *parameter-override* is just a constant expression that evaluates the parameter override value.

Consider the following example, where the parameters within module instance mosekv are changed during instantiation:

```
module cmos_invertor (in, out, dt, vdd, vss);

    inout in, out, dt, vdd;
    electrical in, out, vdd, vss;
    thermal dt;

    parameter real WP = 60.0u;
    parameter real WN = 30.0u;
    parameter real LP = 0.15u;
    parameter real LN = 0.15u;

    mosekv #("PMOS", WP, LP, -0.4, -1.5e-3)
            mp (out, in, vdd, vdd, dt);

    mosekv #("NMOS", WN, LN, 0.4, 1.5e-3)
            mn (out, in, vss, vss, dt);

endmodule
```

It is not necessary to assign values to all of the parameters within a module when using this method. However, the leftmost parameter assignments cannot be skipped. Therefore, to assign values to a subset of the parameters declared within a module, the declarations of the parameters which make up this subset shall precede the declarations of the remaining (optional) parameters. An alternative is to assign values to all of the parameters, but use the default values (the same values assigned in the declaration of the parameters in the module definition) for those parameters which do not need new values.

Hierarchical Parameter Override

Parameter values can be overridden in any module instance throughout the design using the defparam statement:

defparam *def-parameter-override, ...* ;

    where *def-parameter-override* is the hierarchical parameter assignment:

hierarchical-parameter-name = constant-expression

    The *hierarchical-parameter-name* is a hierarchical name of the parameter and the constant expression shall involve only constant numbers and references to parameters declared in the same module as the defparam statement.

    The defparam statement is particularly useful for grouping all of the parameter value override assignments together in one module.

```
module tgate ();
    electrical io1,io2,control,control_bar;
    mosn m1 (io1, io2, control);
    mosp m2 (io1, io2, control_bar);
endmodule

module mosp (drain,gate,source);
    inout drain, gate, source;
    electrical drain, gate, source;
```

```
    parameter gate_length = 0.3e-6,
            gate_width = 4.0e-6;
    spice_pmos #(.l(gate_length),.w(gate_width))
            p (drain, gate, source);
endmodule

module mosn (drain,gate,source);
    inout drain, gate, source;
    electrical drain, gate, source;
    parameter gate_length = 0.3e-6,
            gate_width = 4.0e-6;
    spice_nmos #(.l(gate_length),.w(gate_width))
            n (drain, gate, source);
endmodule

module annotate ();
    defparam
        tgate.m1.gate_width = 5e-6,
        tgate.m2.gate_width = 10e-6;
endmodule
```

If a defparam override conflicts with a module instance parameter override, the parameter in the module shall take the value specified by the defparam override.

Hierarchical System Parameters

In addition to the parameters explicitly declared in a module definition, there are six system parameters that are implicitly declared for every module: $mfactor, $xposition, $yposition, $angle, $hflip, and $vflip. The values of these parameters may be accessed in a module (or paramsets, introduced in the next chapter) using their system names.

The module's value of implicit parameters also propagates to any module instantiated by that module. The top-level value is the starting value at the top of the hierarchy. The hierarchical system parameter names, their top-level values, and allowed values are summarized in Table 5-1.

Table 5-1. *Hierarchical system parameters*

Implicit Parameter	Top-Level Value	Allowed Values
$mfactor	1.0	$mfactor > 0
$xposition	0.0 m	Any
$yposition	0.0 m	Any
$angle	0 deg	$0 \leq \$angle < 360$
$hflip	+1	+1 or −1
$vflip	+1	+1 or −1

$mfactor is the shunt multiplicity factor of the instance. The behavior of the instantiated module in the design is identical to the behavior of the $mfactor of identical modules with the same connections. However, the simulator only has to evaluate the module once. Verilog-A does not provide a method to disable the automatic $mfactor scaling. The simulator shall issue a warning if it detects misuse of the $mfactor in a manner that would result in double-scaling.

The values of the five geometrical system parameters, $xposition, $yposition, $angle, $hflip, and $vflip, do not have any automatic effect on the simulation. The module (or a paramset) may use the values of these parameters to compute geometric layout–dependent effects. $xposition and $yposition are the offsets, in meters, of the location of the center of the instance. $hflip and $vflip are used to indicate that the instance has been mirrored about its center, and $angle indicates that the instance has been rotated some number of degrees in the counterclockwise directions. Note that $angle is specified and returned in degrees, but the built-in math trigonometric functions operate in radians.

The values of hierarchical system parameters may be overridden using an instance parameter override by name, the defparam statement, or a paramset. In all three methods, the system parameter identifier is prefixed by a period (.), just as for explicitly declared parameters. Hierarchical implicit parameters can also be used in parameter alias declarations. The value returned for each hierarchical parameter is computed by combining values from the top of the hierarchy down to the instance using the parameter. If a module is instantiated without specifying a value of one of these system parameters, then the value of that system parameter will be unchanged from the instantiating module. If a value is specified, then its value is obtained by combining the value specified for the instance and the value obtained by traversing the hierarchy from the top to the instantiating module. The values of $mfactor, $hflip, and $vflip are hierarchically combined by multiplication while the values of $xposition, $yposition, and $angle by addition.

In the following example, the top-level module is used to override the values of hierarchical parameters $mfactor and $xposition in the instantiating test_module:

```
module top();
    defparam
        test_module.$mfactor = 3,
        test_module.$xposition = 1.1u;
endmodule

module test_module(p,n);
    inout p,n;
    electrical p,n;
    module_a A1(p,n);
endmodule
```

```
module module_a(p,n);
    inout p,n;
    electrical p,n;
    module_b #(.$mfactor(2)
               .$xposition(1u)) B1(p,n);
endmodule

module module_b(p,n);
    inout p,n;
    electrical p,n;
    module_c #(.$mfactor(5)
               .$xposition(2u)) C1(p,n);
endmodule
```

The values of the hierarchical system parameters $mfactor and $xposition in the module instance test_module.A1.B1.C1 are 30 and 4.1u, respectively.

CHAPTER 6

Paramsets

Paramset is a powerful Verilog-A language construct providing a convenient way to collect common parameter overrides for a specific component technology and define it independently of a particular system design. The paramsets are not only removing the redundancy in parameter overrides for multiple instances of the same module but they are also promoting the exchange of common parameter overrides among different designs.

Introducing Paramsets

The module instantiation often requires long lists of instance parameter overrides with a lot of redundancy among instances of the same module. Take, for example, compact models of transistors in electronic circuit design. Customization of the compact transistor models to certain device geometry and fabrication technology typically requires a large number of parameter overrides. But most of the technology-related parameter overrides will be identical for all instances of transistors realized with the same process technology. Only a few parameter overrides (typically related to a device geometry and surrounding) could be specific for a particular transistor instance. Paramsets can resolve this issue by specifying parameter overrides once to be shared between many instances of the same module. The concept of paramset is not quite new. The shared storage of parameter overrides for multiple instances makes them very

© Slobodan Mijalković 2022
S. Mijalković, *A Practical Guide to Verilog-A*, https://doi.org/10.1007/978-1-4842-6351-8_6

similar to the SPICE simulator's model card. Verilog-A simulators are expected to optimize the storage of paramset values in a manner similar to the way SPICE optimizes model parameter storage.

Paramsets are defined as separate entities from the modules but each paramset must be hierarchically associated with a module or another paramset as shown in Figure 6-1.

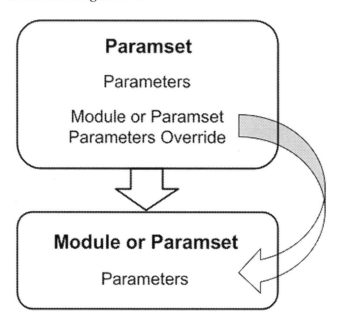

Figure 6-1. *A paramset and associated parent module or paramset*

A hierarchy of paramsets may be defined in this way. However, a module shall always be at the bottom of the hierarchy. The only restriction imposed on such a parent module is that it should not contain a `defparam` statement in or under its hierarchy.

The paramsets contain no behavioral code. All of the behavioral descriptions can be only defined in the module at the bottom of the paramset hierarchy. However, paramset can override the parameters of the parent module. Moreover, a paramset may declare its own parameters that may be overridden in the child paramsets.

The main benefit of having paramsets as collections of parent module parameter overrides is the possibility to replace the instantiation of a parent module with the instantiation of the associated paramset as shown in Figure 6-2.

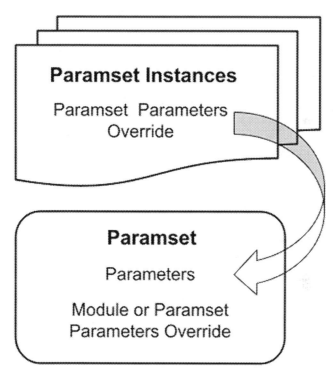

Figure 6-2. *Paramset instantiation*

Instantiation of a paramset is practically identical to the instantiation of its parent module except that it is not necessary anymore to provide a list of module parameter overrides since they are already defined in the paramset. All instances of the same paramset share the same collection of parent module parameter overrides. A simulator can use this information to optimize data storage for the instances.

The paramset instances may only provide overrides for their own parameters. The overridden paramset parameters can be used in the paramset definition to customize the override of related parent module parameters specific to a particular instance.

Paramsets can be also used to assign or override the values of the parent module output variables. This paramset feature is discussed in more detail in Chapter 18.

Defining Paramsets

A paramset definition is enclosed between the keywords `paramset` and `endparamset` using the syntax:

```
paramset paramset-name module-or-paramset-name ;
        paramset-statement ...
endparamset
```

The keyword `paramset` in the header line, ending with a semicolon (`;`), is followed by a unique identifier *paramset-name*, defining the name of the paramset, and identifier *module-or-paramset-name*, which shall be the name of a module or paramset with which the paramset is associated. The paramset body, between the header line and the keyword `endparamset`, contains a sequence of statements permitted in paramsets. The principle statements permitted in paramsets are parameter declaration and parameter override statements.

Paramset Parameters

Paramsets permit the declaration of parameters, including local parameters and parameter aliases. Here are examples of parameter declaration in paramsets `most`, `nch_most`, and `pch_most` hierarchically associated with the `mosekv` module:

```
paramset most mosekv;
   parameter string MTYP = "NMOS";
   parameter real LEFF = 0.15u;
   parameter real WEFF = 1u;
   parameter integer SHMOD = 0;
endparamset

paramset nch_most most;
   parameter real LEFF = 0.15u;
   parameter real WEFF = 1u;
   localparam real AREA = LEFF * WEFF from [0:1p)
endparamset

paramset pch_most most;
   parameter real LEFF = 0.15u;
   parameter real WEFF = 1u;
   aliasparam L=LEFF, W = WEFF;
endparamset
```

The parameter declarations in paramsets follow the same syntax as the parameter declarations inside modules. However, the paramset parameters are not related in any way to the parameters declared in the parent module or parent paramset. For example, the paramset parameters LEFF and WEFF in the nch_most are independent of the parameters declared with the same names in the most paramset and the mosekv module. The paramset parameters can be used only in the scope of the paramset where they are declared. However, paramset parameters play a special role in the process of paramset resolution.

Parameter Override Statements

The paramset override statement is used to modify the default values of the parent module or paramset non-local parameters. It is defined with the syntax:

. *parent_parameter_name* = constant-expression ;

All of the parent non-local parameters, including hierarchical system parameters, are accessible for override from within the paramset by preceding their names by the period (.). The constant expression on the right-hand side can be composed of basic type literals, parameters, and hierarchical out-of-module references to local parameters of a different module. Hierarchical out-of-module references to non-local parameters of a different module are not allowed in parameter override statements. If a paramset override statement assigns a new value to a parameter in the parent module or paramset, and this value is outside the range specified for that module parameter, it shall be an error.

The following example illustrates the usage of parameter override statements in the hierarchy of paramsets nch_most and pch_most defined over the paramset most associated with the mosekv module:

```
paramset nch_most most;
    parameter real LEFF = 0.15u;
    parameter real WEFF = 1u;
    localparam real AREA = LEFF * WEFF from [0:1p)

    .LEFF=LEFF;
    .WEFF=WEFF;
endparamset

paramset pch_most most;
    parameter real LEFF = 0.15u;
    parameter real WEFF = 1u;
    aliasparam L=LEFF, W = WEFF;
```

```
    .MTYP="PMOS";
    .LEFF=LEFF;
    .WEFF=WEFF;
endparamset

paramset most mosekv;
    parameter string MTYP = "NMOS";
    parameter real LEFF = 0.15u;
    parameter real WEFF = 1u;
    parameter integer SHMOD = 0;

    .TYPE=MTYP;
    .LEFF=LEFF;
    .WEFF=WEFF;
    .SHMOD=SHMOD;

    .VTO = 0.5;
    .TCV = 1.6m;
    .PHI=1.05;
    .GAMMA=0.8;
    .KP=tech.uO * `P_EPSO * tech.eps_r / tech.tox ;
    .THETA=48.0e-3;
    .BEX=-1.8;
    .mfactor = 1.0;
endparamset

module tech;
    localparam real tox = 3e-8; // oxide depth
    local parameter real eps_r=11.7;
    local parameter real uO = 3e-2; // mobility
endmodule
```

The module tech is a top-level module, created as a commonplace for physical and technology constants used in paramset override statements. Such a module is often referred to as a constant module. The declaration of local parameters in the tech module is essential if their hierarchical references are used in paramset override statements.

The parameter override expression may also use the stochastic built-in functions as long as the arguments to these functions are constant. This possibility to use paramset in probabilistic simulations will be discussed in Chapter 10.

Other Paramset Statements

Paramsets permit also declarations of numerical (integer or real) basic type variables and limited use of procedural statements. The restrictions on the procedural statements permitted in paramsets are similar to the restrictions for statements in user-defined functions introduced in Chapter 11. The values assigned to paramset basic type variables need not be constant. However, these variables shall not be used in the parameter override statements. They are mainly used to assign and override module output variables, as described in Chapter 18.

Paramset Instantiation

Instantiation of a paramset basically instantiates its parent module with all parameter overrides previously defined in the associated paramset hierarchy. The parent module parameters that are not overridden in paramsets are assigned the default values given in the parent module parameter declarations. The paramset and module instantiation statements use the same syntax. However, the paramset instantiation statement may override only the non-local paramset parameters.

The example of the cmos_invertor module, introduced in the previous chapter, is rewritten here using paramset instead of the module instantiation statements:

```
module cmos_invertor (in, out, dt, vdd, vss);

    inout in, out, dt, vdd;
    electrical in, out, vdd, vss;
    thermal dt;

    parameter real WP = 60.0u;
    parameter real WN = 30.0u;
    parameter real LP = 0.15u;
    parameter real LN = 0.15u;

    pch_most #(.W(WP),
                .L(LP))
                mp (out, in, vdd, vdd, dt);

    nch_most #(.WEFF(WN),
                .LEFF(LN))
                mn (out, in, vss, vss, dt);
endmodule
```

It is also possible to use instance paramset parameter override by order:

```
...
pch_most #(LP,WP) mp (out, in, vdd, vdd, dt);
nch_most #(LN,WN) mn (out, in, vss, vss, dt);
...
```

following the order of their declaration in the paramset definition. The paramset instances override now only two paramset parameters WEFF and LEFF. Note that the alias parameter declarations in the pch_most module allow using W and L instead of WEFF and LEFF for paramset parameter override. An attempt to override any of the other parameters of the parent paramset most or the parent module mosekv would generate an error.

Paramset names need not be unique in paramset instantiation statements. Multiple paramsets can be declared using the same paramset name, and they may refer to different modules or parent paramsets. During elaboration, the simulator shall choose an appropriate paramset from the set that shares a given name for every instance that references that name. When choosing an appropriate paramset, the following paramset resolution steps shall be enforced:

1. For each instance, find all paramsets for which

   a. All parameters overridden on the instance are parameters of the paramset.

   b. The parameters of the paramset, with overrides and defaults, are all within the allowed ranges specified in the paramset parameter declaration.

   c. The local parameters of the paramset, computed from parameters, are within the allowed range specified in the paramset.

   d. The underlying module has a port declared for each port connected to the instance line.

2. Choose the paramset which has the fewest number of un-overridden parameters.

3. Choose the paramset with the greatest number of local parameters with specified ranges.

4. Choose the paramset with the fewest ports not connected in the instance line.

It shall be an error if there is still more than one applicable paramset for an instance after the application of this algorithm.

The following example illustrates some of the rules for paramset selection. Consider a design that includes the following paramsets:

```
paramset nch_most most; // with SHMOD parameter
    parameter real LEFF = 0.15u;
    parameter real WEFF = 1u;
    parameter integer SHMOD = 0;

    .LEFF=LEFF;
    .WEFF=WEFF;
    .SHMOD=SHMOD;
endparamset

paramset nch_most most; // with local parameter
    parameter real LEFF = 0.15u;
    parameter real WEFF = 1u;
    localparam real AREA = LEFF * WEFF from [0:1p)

    .LEFF=LEFF;
    .WEFF=WEFF;
endparamset

paramset nch_most most; // short-channel paramset
    parameter real LEFF = 0.15u from [0.25u:1u);
    parameter real WEFF = 1u;

    .LEFF=LEFF;
    .WEFF=WEFF;
endparamset

paramset nch_most most; // long-channel paramset
    parameter real LEFF = 1u from [1u:inf);
    parameter real WEFF = 1u;
```

```
    .LEFF=LEFF;
    .WEFF=WEFF;
endparamset
```

The following instances might exist in the design:

```
nch_most #(.WEFF(2u),.LEFF(0.5u),.SHMOD(1))
        m1 (out, in, vss, vss, dt);
nch_most #(.WEFF(1u),.LEFF(0.5u))
        m2 (out, in, vss, vss, dt);
nch_most #(.WEFF(3u),.LEFF(0.5u))
        m3 (out, in, vss, vss, dt);
nch_most #(.WEFF(1u),.LEFF(5u))
        m4 (out, in, vss, vss, dt);
```

The instance m1 will use the paramset with the SHMOD parameter because it is the only one for which SHMOD is a parameter. This paramset cannot be selected by other instances because it will have always one un-overridden parameter. The instance m2 will use the paramset defined with a local parameter, because it has local parameters with defined ranges and the short-channel paramset not, and the LEFF parameter is out of range for the long-channel paramset. The instance m3 will use the short-channel paramset because the evaluated value of AREA in the paramset with the local parameter will be out of range as well as LEFF parameter in the long-channel paramset. The instance m4 will use the long-channel paramset because the AREA local parameters and LEFF parameter will be out of range in paramsets with local parameter and short-channel paramset.

CHAPTER 7

Procedural Programming

The backbone of behavioral description and data manipulation in the Verilog-A language is procedural programming. It resembles in many ways programming languages that declare a set of variables and use a sequence of procedural statements to execute certain computations or algorithms. While variables may be declared along with parameters in the module body, the procedural statements in Verilog-A are encapsulated within procedural blocks. This chapter introduces the procedural blocks and procedural statements for variable assignment and control flow. The control flow statements allow selection between alternative courses as well as repetition of procedural statement execution.

Variables

Similar to parameters, variables are containers for basic type values. Apart from the parameters, being runtime constants, variables can be used to store intermediary results in procedural programming.

Before any variable can be used in expressions and procedural statements, it shall be declared. The general syntax for the variable declaration statement is

```
basic-type variable-declarator, ... ;
```

© Slobodan Mijalković 2022
S. Mijalković, *A Practical Guide to Verilog-A*, https://doi.org/10.1007/978-1-4842-6351-8_7

The *basic-type* determines the variable type and may be one of the keywords integer, real, and string. It is followed by a list of variable declarators that can specify variables as simple or array variables and can also provide variable initial values.

Simple Variables

The *variable-declarator* for simple variables is just an identifier representing the variable name:

```
integer count;
real alpha;
string name;
```

It is possible to declare several simple variables in a single declaration statement using a list of comma-separated identifiers:

```
integer index, dmax;
string name1, name2, name3;
```

Another way to declare multiple data of the same basic type is to use array variables.

The simple variables can be also initialized (assigned an initial value) in their declaration statements using variable assignment construct:

```
variable-name = constant-expression
```

as the *variable-declarator*. The initial value can be any expression that evaluates a basic type constant:

```
integer count = 0, dmax = 15;
real alpha = 2.5;
string my_daughter_name = "Jona";
```

If an initial value is not specified, integer or real variables are initialized to zero (0). The initial value for string variables can be a string literal or a string-type constant expression. If an initial value is not specified for a string variable, it is initialized to an empty string " ".

Array Variables

An array variable is a collection of data elements having the same basic type. Array variables are declared using a construct:

variable-name range ...

as the *variable-declarator*, where one or more range specifiers are added after a variable name. The number of range specifiers defines array variable dimensionality. Here is an example of a one-dimensional string array variable:

```
string name [1:3];
```

Multidimensional arrays are represented as arrays of arrays by successively specifying the dimension ranges after the variable name:

```
integer d2 [0:7][0:3];
real d3 [1:50][1:20][5:10];
```

The two-dimensional array d2 consists of 8 one-dimensional arrays with 4 integer elements, while the three-dimensional array d3 consists of 50 elements that are two-dimensional arrays.

The initial values for array variables are introduced using the extended array variable declarator:

variable-name range ... = constant-assignment-pattern

where the assignment pattern at the right-hand side contains only constant basic type expressions: ,

```
integer n[1:2][1:3]='{ '{0,1,2}, '{4,4,3} };
real poles[0:3]='{ 1.0, 3.198, 4.554, 2.00 };
string names[1:3] = '{ "first", "middle", "last" };
```

Note the use of nested assignment patterns for initialization of two-dimensional array variable n. It provides a clear correspondence between array ranges and a collection of expressions in the assignment pattern.

Procedural Blocks

Procedural blocks encapsulate procedural statements within the Verilog-A module definitions. It is essentially based on analog blocks and block procedural statements.

Analog Blocks

A procedural block is introduced into module definition using the analog construct:

```
analog procedural-statement
```

where the analog keyword is followed by a definition of executable *procedural-statement*. The basic procedural statements could be assignment and control flow programming statements described later in this chapter. However, branch contribution, event control, and system task statements, introduced in the following chapters, can be also used as procedural statements in analog blocks. A procedural statement in an analog procedural block is executed at every point during simulation when variables or signals referenced from the procedural statement are changed.

For the purpose of simulation initialization, Verilog-A provides also a special analog initial construct:

```
analog initial procedural-statement
```

where the keyword `initial` is inserted after the keyword `analog`. The initial block procedural statement is executed once before the simulation starts. At that point, values of net signals are not yet available which restricts the procedural statements in analog initial blocks to the basic programming and system task procedural statements. An analog initial procedural block shall be re-executed whenever a variable that is referenced from its procedural statement is changed during simulation.

A module may have multiple analog and analog initial blocks that shall be executed in the order they appear in the module definition. Since the sequence of analog and analog initial blocks are executed separately, they can be mixed in a module definition. Syntactically, analog blocks consist of a single procedural statement. However, *procedural-statement* stands also for a block or compound procedural statement. The block statements are grouping multiple statements, including other block statements so that they can be treated as one statement. The use of a single block procedural statement in an analog construct is a common practice that also justifies the name *analog block* used for such constructs.

Block Procedural Statements

In the simplest case, a block procedural statement is defined as a sequence of procedural statements enclosed by the `begin` and `end` keywords:

```
begin
  procedural-statement ...
end
```

A block statement does not perform any functionality in itself but is used to group two or more procedural statements so that they can be treated as a single procedural statement. A procedural block with a single procedural statement can be used without the `begin` and `end` keywords.

The block procedural statement can be used anywhere a single procedural statement is allowed and can be nested inside other block procedural statements. During the simulation, the procedural statements within the block statement shall be executed in sequence, one after another in the given order, and the control shall pass out of the block after the last statement is executed.

Verilog-A permits also a named block procedural statement using the syntax:

```
begin : block-name
    variable-or-parameter-declaration ...
    procedural-statement ...
end
```

where a colon character (:) and identifier *block-name* are added after the keyword `begin`. Note that the naming of a procedural block statement allows variables and parameters to be declared for that block which is not allowed in unnamed procedural blocks. The named procedural block statement introduces a new scope in the module hierarchy as a region where declared variables and parameters can have existence and beyond which cannot be directly accessed. However, the block names give a means of uniquely accessing all locally defined variables and parameters in the named block by their hierarchical names. In the `test_scope` module example:

```
module test_scope;
    parameter integer p1 = 1;
    real moduleVar;
    analog begin
```

```
    begin: myscope
        parameter real p2 = p1;
        real localVar = 1.5 * p2;
    end
    moduleVar = myscope.localVar;
  end
endmodule
```

it will be an error to access the variable localVar outside the named procedural block myscope where it is defined. But it can be still accessed in the module scope using the hierarchical name myscope.localVar. The block variables are often referred to as local variables in relation to global module scope variables. The local variables in Verilog-A are static, that is, a unique location exists for all variables, and leaving or entering the block does not affect the values stored in them. Local variables cannot be assigned outside the scope of the block in which they are declared.

Parameters declared within a named block have local scope and cannot be assigned outside the scope. An instance parameter override can only affect parameters declared at module scope. For example, in the top module:

```
module top;
  test_scope #(.p1(4)) inst1();          // allowed
  test_scope #(.myscope.p2(4)) inst2(); // error endmodule
```

it is an error to attempt the instance override of the block parameter p2.

Assignment Statements

An assignment statement sets and resets values stored in the variables in the procedural blocks.

Scalar Assignments

The declared basic type variables are containers for the basic type values. To change the data value stored in a variable, we use the equal sign (=) in the assignment statement:

variable-name = `expression`;

which sets or resets the data value of the identifier *variable-name*, on the left to the basic type value produced by the expression on the right.

The equal sign (=) is not an operator in the Verilog-A language. It performs the assignment operation but does not return a value. It cannot be used as an operand in the expressions:

```
a = b = 0.5; // Chained assignments are not possible
```

Also, it cannot be used in combination with other operators as a compound assignment operator:

```
a += 1; // Compound assignments are not possible
```

Variables can be assigned initial values in their declaration statement and reassigned in procedural statements.

Procedural assignments are used for updating the variable values during the execution of the Verilog-A models:

```
real vt, ratio, vto_th;
int A[10:1];
...
vt = `P_K * temp / `P_Q + 1.0e-6;
ratio = abs(temp / tempref + 1.0e-6);
vto_th = MTYP * (VTO - TCV * (temp - tempref));
A[5] = 1.0;
```

The assigned can be any arbitrary expression, although some restrictions may apply depending on the context in which the procedural assignment is used.

If the type of the variable is declared as integer or real, and the value assigned to the variable conflicts with the declared variable type, the value is converted to the type of the variable if it is possible:

```
integer i, k;
...
i = 3.14;       // real truncated to integer
k = 2.9979e40; // undefined
```

In the first case, the real constant is truncated and 3 is assigned to i. The result in the second case is undefined since an integer cannot hold such a large value. It shall be an error to assign a numeric value to a variable declared as a string or to assign a string value to a real variable.

A string literal assigned to an integral variable of a different size is either truncated to the size of the variable or padded with zeros to the left as necessary. If a string literal is assigned to a string variable, the size of the variable is adjusted so that neither the literal is truncated nor the variable is padded with zeros.

Array Assignments

Verilog-A also supports array assignment statements:

```
int A[10:1], B[0:9], C[24:1];
...
A = B; // ok. Compatible type and same size
A = C; // type-check error: different sizes
```

where arrays are used on the right-hand side of the assignment statement.

Array assignments shall only be done with compatible arrays. An array, or a slice of such an array, shall be assignment compatible with any other such array or slice if all the following conditions are satisfied:

- The array on the left-hand side of the assignment shall be an array variable, a slice of an array variable.

- The basic types of the source and target arrays shall be equivalent.

- Every dimension of the source array shall have the same number of elements as the target array.

The array assignment cannot be used for array variable initialization. This can be only achieved using assignment patterns.

Conditional Statements

The model evaluation often depends on conditions that may or may not hold during the simulation. There are two types of conditional statements in Verilog-A: if and case statements.

if Statement

The if statement is defined using the basic syntax:

```
if ( condition ) procedural-statement
```

or the extended syntax with the else clause:

```
if ( condition )
    procedural-statement-1
else
    procedural-statement-2
```

The latter is also known as the if-else statement. The *condition* is any valid expression that produces a numeric value. If the *condition* value is nonzero, the *procedural-statement*, or *procedural-statement-1*, if an else clause is used, is executed. Otherwise, only the *procedural-statement-2* is executed.

For example, the following if statements:

```
if (i != 0) x = 1.0;
if (i == 0) x = 2.0;
```

can be combined into a single if statement with an else clause:

```
if (i != 0) x = 1.0 else x = 2.0;
```

Since the if statement simply tests the nonzero status of the *condition* expression, certain shortcuts are possible. For example, the preceding code fragments can be also written (perhaps more obscurely) as

```
if (i) x = 1.0 else x = 2.0;
```

The conditionally executed statements can be null. However, if any of the conditionally executed statements contains an analog operator, the *condition* expression shall be a constant expression.

Because the else part of an if-else is optional, there can be confusion when an else is omitted from a nested if statement sequence. This is resolved by always associating the else clause with the closest previous if statement which lacks an else.

In the following example, the else goes with the inner if statement, as shown by indentation:

```
if (index > 0)
    if (i > j)
        result = i;
    else // else applies to preceding if
        result = j;
```

If that association is not desired, a begin-end block shall be used to force the proper association, as shown in the following:

```
if (index > 0) begin
    if (i > j)
        result = i;
    end
    else result = j;
```

Nesting of if statements (known as an if-else-if construct) is the most general way of writing a multi-way decision. The expressions are evaluated in order. If any if statement *condition* is nonzero, the procedural statement associated with it shall be executed and this action shall terminate the whole chain.

case **Statement**

The case statement takes a general form:

```
case  ( case-expression )
    case-item, ... : procedural-statement
    case-item, ... : procedural-statement
    ...
    default : procedural-statement
endcase
```

The case statement is a multi-way decision statement that tests if an expression matches one of some other expressions and, if so, branches accordingly. The default statement is optional. The use of multiple default statements in one case statement is illegal.

The *case-expression* and the *case-item* expression can be computed at runtime; neither expression is required to be a constant expression.

The *case-expression* and *case-item* expressions are evaluated and compared in the exact order in which they are given. During this linear search, if one of the *case-item* expressions matches the *case-expression* given in parentheses, then the procedural or block statement associated with that *case-item* is executed. If all comparisons fail, and the default item is given, then the default item statement is executed; otherwise, none of the *case-item* procedural statements are executed. Here is an example of how the case statement can be used:

```
case(rgeo)
    1, 2, 5:
        get_rendi = rsh * dmcg / (weffcj * nuend);
    3, 4, 6:
        get_rendi = rsh * weffcj /
                        (3.0 * nuend * (dmcg + dmci));
    default:
    $strobe("specified rgeo = %d not matched", rgeo);
endcase
```

Looping Statements

In the procedural Verilog-A code, it is often necessary to execute one or more statements many times. It is tedious to repeat the statements and, in any case, it is often impossible to predict how many times the execution should be repeated. Such circumstances are handled by the three looping statements: for, while, and repeat. These statements provide a means of controlling the execution of a procedural statement zero, one, or more times.

Looping statements shall not contain analog operators, event control statements, and branch contribution statements.

while Statement

The while statement has a syntax:

```
while ( control ) procedural-statement
```

The expression *control*, which is of a numeric type, is evaluated before each execution of the *procedural-statement*. The *procedural-statement* is executed if the *control* is evaluated as nonzero and then the test of the *control* expression is repeated. This cycle continues until *control* becomes zero, at which point execution resumes after *procedural-statement*. A single execution of the loop body is called an iteration. If the test never fails, then the iteration never terminates:

```
integer n = 1;
while (n > 0)
    begin
      gamma = gamma * n;
      n = n + 1;
    end
```

The while statements are typically used for iterative processes as in the following example:

```
real b = 1.0, c = 2.0, x = 0.0;
integer niter = 0;
while ( niter < 100 )
    begin
        x = (x**3 - c) / b;
        niter = niter + 1;
    end
```

that implements a simple fixed-point iterative method for solving the cubic equation: $x^3 - bx - c = 0$.

for Statement

The for statement has a syntax:

```
for ( initialization ; control ; change ) procedural-statement
```

that is equivalent to

```
initialization ;
while ( control ) begin
    procedural-statement
        change ;
end
```

and whether to use for-loop or its while-loop equivalent formulation is largely a matter of personal preference.

The for-loop statement employs three actions, which are called *initialization*, *control*, and *change*, to indicate their respective roles in the conditional execution of *procedural-statement*. The *initialization* executes a variable assignment operation, normally used to initialize an integer index variable that controls the number of executed loops with the procedural statement. The *control* evaluates an expression, and if the result is nonzero, the for-loop statement executes *procedural-statement*, and otherwise the for-loop exits. The *change* executes a variable assignment, normally used to modify the value of the loop control index variable, and if the *control* is still nonzero, *procedural-statement* is executed again. The for statement continues to cycle between the *control*, *procedural-statement*, and *change* until the *control* expression is zero. The control then passes beyond the for-loop statement. In the following example:

```
for (i = 0; i < B4SOInf; i = i+1)
    begin : summation
        real T0;
        T0 = 1.0 / B4SOInf / (B4SOIsa
```

```
                + 0.5 * Ldrn + i * (B4SOIsd + Ldrn));
        Inv_sa = Inv_sa + TO;
    end
```

the for-loop statement is used to accumulate multiple contributions to the variable Inv_sa.

It is worth noting that there are no restrictions on the numerical type of the control variable and *control* expression to evaluate as integers; they can be also of real type:

```
for (x = 0.0; x != 10; x = x + 1.0)
    total = total + x;
```

However, a test for equality of real type is very risky since it is likely that the finite machine precision will mean that the condition never occurs. For this reason, it is very unusual to have a loop counter and *control* expression which is a real type.

repeat **Statement**

The repeat statement has the syntax:

```
repeat ( number ) procedural-statement
```

It executes a *procedural-statement* a fixed number of times. Evaluation of the expression *number* determines how many times a procedural statement is executed:

```
i = 0;
repeat (NF-1)
    begin
        T1 = T1 + 1.0 / (SA + 0.5 * L
            + i * (SD + L))
            + 1.0 / (SB + 0.5 * L
```

```
          + i * (SD + L));
    i = i + 1;
end
```

The expression *number* shall be evaluated once before the execution of any statement to determine the number of times, if any, the statements are executed.

CHAPTER 8

Branches

A behavioral description of an analog system is constructed as a network of interconnected branches. The constitutive equations of the system component are formulated in terms of branch potential and flow signals. This chapter describes how to declare branches as well as how to access and contribute branch signals.

Declaring Branches

A branch is a path between two nets representing branch terminals. A branch can only be declared inside a module scope along with net and port declarations and not in named procedural blocks. The branches can be declared as scalar or vector branches. It is also possible to declare a special type of port branch.

Scalar Branches

The scalar branches are declared using the statement:

```
branch ( scalar-terminal , scalar-terminal ) branch-name, ... ;
```

© Slobodan Mijalković 2022
S. Mijalković, *A Practical Guide to Verilog-A*, https://doi.org/10.1007/978-1-4842-6351-8_8

where the keyword branch is followed by the specification of the branch terminals in the parentheses and a list of identifiers representing branch names. The *scalar-terminal* can be a scalar net or an element of a vector net:

```
electrical p;
voltage n;
kinematic [1:3] x;
...
branch (p, n) b;
branch (x[1], x[2]) d12;
```

It is also possible to use hierarchical scalar net references as scalar terminals:

```
branch (x[3], top.drv.y) d3
```

The disciplines for the specified scalar terminals shall be compatible.

The scalar branch declaration statement can specify a single scalar terminal:

```
branch ( scalar-terminal ) branch-name, ... ;
```

In that case, the second scalar terminal defaults to the ground net:

```
thermal dt;
...
branch (dt) rth, cth;
```

Here, the branches rth and cth are declared between dt and ground nets of the thermal discipline.

Vector Branches

Multiple branches can be declared using a vector branch declaration statement:

```
branch ( vector-terminal , vector-terminal ) branch-name, ... ;
```

where vector terminals are used instead of the scalar ones. Vector terminals can be local or hierarchical vector nets that are compatible and of the same size:

```
electrical [5:3] a;
voltage [1:3] b;
...
branch (a, b) vb;
```

The multiple scalar branches that make the vector branch connect to the corresponding scalar nets of the vector terminals, as shown in Figure 8-1.

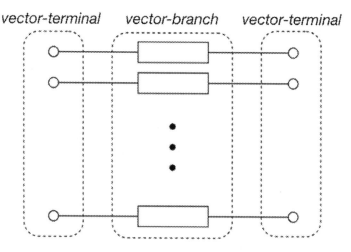

Figure 8-1. *A vector branch with two vector terminals*

For example, the scalar branch components of the vector branch vb are (a[5],b[1]), (a[4],b[2]), and (a[3],b[3]).

Vector branches can be also declared using vector net slices as vector terminals:

```
branch (a[5:4], b[1:2]) vb1;
```

A vector slice is a set of consecutive vector elements selected by the range after the vector net name.

The indexing of the declared vector branches shall start at 0. It can be changed by adding a range after the branch name:

```
branch (a[5:4], b[1:2]) vb2 [1:2];
```

Both vb1 and vb2 are declared as vector branches of size 2, but vb1 is indexed from 0 to 1 while vb2 from 1 to 2.

The vector branches can be declared with one of the terminals being a scalar terminal:

```
branch ( vector-terminal , scalar-terminal ) branch-name, ... ;
branch ( scalar-terminal , vector-terminal ) branch-name, ... ;
```

In that case, scalar branches that make the vector branch connect each element of the vector terminal to the scalar terminal, as shown in Figure 8-2.

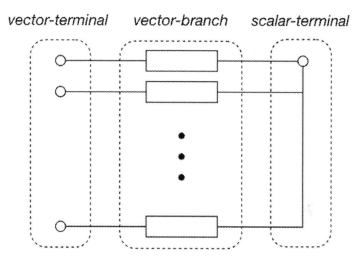

vector-terminal   vector-branch   scalar-terminal

Figure 8-2. *A vector branch with a vector and a scalar terminal*

The vector branch declaration statement can specify only one vector terminal:

branch (*vector-terminal*) *branch-name, ... ;*

The second implicit terminal is assumed to be the scalar ground net.

Port Branches

A port branch is a special type of branch between the upper and lower connections of the port. A declaration statement for port branches has the syntax:

branch (< *port-reference* >) *branch-name, ... ;*

where *port-reference* is a local or hierarchical port identifier. It shall be enclosed between < and > characters:

```
inout electrical p;
inout electrical [2:4] vp;
...
branch (<p>) b;
branch (<vp>) vb [1:3]
```

A port branch is a scalar or vector branch if the port is a scalar or vector port, respectively. An optional range specifier can be used after the declared vector ports. Otherwise, the indexing of the declared vector port branches shall start at 0.

Branch Signals

A branch is associated with potential and flow signals based on the terminal disciplines. If both branch terminals are conservative, then the branch is conservative and it defines both a branch potential and a branch flow. If one of the branch terminals is a signal-flow net, then the branch is a signal-flow branch and it is characterized by either a branch potential or a branch flow, but not both. Signal access functions are used to access branch signal values.

Signal Directions

Verilog-A uses associated potential and flow signal directions. For a branch between scalar terminals p and n:

```
branch (p, n) b;
```

the potential and flow signal directions are associated as shown in Figure 8-3.

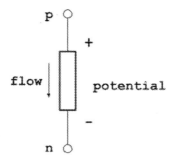

Figure 8-3. *Branch potential and flow directions*

The direction for potential is indicated by the plus and minus signs at branch terminals. The branch potential is positive whenever the potential of the first declared branch terminal, marked with a plus sign, is larger than the potential of the second declared branch terminal, marked with a minus sign. The arrow indicates the flow direction. A positive flow enters a branch through the first declared terminal and exits the branch through the second declared terminal.

Signal Access Functions

The values of branch potential and flow signals can be accessed using signal access functions with the syntax:

nature-access-name (*branch-reference*)

The *nature-access-name* identifier must be the value of the access attribute defined in the potential or flow natures for the discipline associated with the branch terminals. As an alternative, the potential and flow keywords can be used as generic signal access function names.

potential (*branch-reference*)
flow (*branch-reference*)

The *branch-reference* is a local or hierarchical name of the branch where the signal is accessed. It shall be a scalar branch or an individual element of a vector branch.

Note   Verilog-A allows ports, nets, and branches to be declared as vector quantities. However, signal access functions can only access a signal of a single branch.

The signal access functions syntactically resemble the function calls, but essentially they are kind of handles for the branch signal values. They can be used in expressions requiring branch signal values. But similar to variables, they can be used to assign signal values in contribution statements.

Table 8-1 shows examples of signal access functions applied to the previously declared scalar branch b, vector branch vb, and port branch p of the electrical discipline.

Table 8-1. *Examples of using signal access functions*

Example	Accessed Signal
V(b) potential(b)	Voltage (potential) of branch b1
I(b) flow(b)	Current (flow) of branch b
V(vb[2]) I(vb[2])	Voltage (current) of the vector branch vb element
V(vb) I(vb)	Error. It is illegal to use vector branches as signal access function arguments
I(p) flow(p)	Current flow into the module through port branch p
V(p) potential(p)	Error. It is illegal to use port branches as arguments in potential access functions

Note that some restrictions apply to the access of port branch signals. It is not allowed to use port branch references with potential signal accessing functions. Only the *nature-access-name* for the flow nature or the flow keyword can be used with port branch references.

It is allowed to access the potential and flow signals of a branch in other module instances using hierarchical branch reference:

```
Temp(top.a1.b)
potential(top.a1.b)
```

Here, branch b is declared in the module instance a1, instantiated in the top module.

Unnamed Branches

The Verilog-A syntax allows signal access functions to use the branch terminal or port references as arguments instead of declared branch names. The branches accessed this way are called unnamed branches. Unnamed branches can be used in addition to any number of named branches declared with the same terminal or port references. The unnamed branch references are specified in the parentheses of the signal access function calls using the syntax:

```
( scalar-terminal , scalar-terminal )
( scalar-terminal )
( < scalar-port-reference > )
```

It is similar to the terminal specification that would be used in branch declarations but restricted to scalar net terminals and ports or scalar elements of the vector nets and ports. If only one scalar terminal is given as the argument to a signal access function, the second terminal of the unnamed branch is assumed to be the ground net.

Table 8-2 shows examples of the signal access functions applied to unnamed branches with scalar terminals n1 and n2 and a scalar port p of the electrical discipline.

Table 8-2. *Examples of using signal access functions with*
unnamed branches

Example	Accessed Signal
V(n1) potential(n1)	Voltage (potential) of the unnamed branch between net n1 and ground net
V(n1) potential(n1,n2)	Voltage (potential) of the unnamed branch between nets n1 and n2
I(n1) flow(n1)	Current (flow) of the unnamed branch from n1 to the ground net
I(n1,n2) flow(n1,n2)	Current (flow) of the unnamed branch between nets n1 and n2
V(n1,n1) potential(n1,n1) I(n1,n1) flow(n1,n1)	Error, there is no branch
I(<p>) flow(<p>)	Current flow into the module through port p
V(<p>) potential(<p>)	Error. It is illegal to use an unnamed port branch as an argument in potential access functions

It is not allowed to use two identical scalar terminals as an unnamed branch and to access the potential signals of an unnamed port branch.

The unnamed branches can be also accessed with hierarchical references. For example:

```
V(top.a1.a, top.a1.k)
```

is accessing the voltage of an unnamed branch between the scalar nets a and k declared in the module instance a1 instantiated in the top module.

Unnamed branches can be also accessed hierarchically using a special syntax:

hierarchical-instance . branch (*scalar_terminal* , *scalar_terminal*)
hierarchical-instance . branch (*scalar_terminal*)
hierarchical-instance . branch (< *scalar-port-reference* >)

where the keyword branch precedes the specification of the unnamed branch in the parentheses. The previous example of a hierarchically accessed unnamed branch voltage can be also expressed as

```
V(top.a1.branch(a,k))
```

It provides a single argument to the signal access functions similar to named branches.

Contributing Branch Signals

Branch potential and flow signal values are assigned with contribution statements. Contribution statements may be described in direct or indirect as well as explicit and implicit forms. Accessing a signal of an unassigned branch creates an implicitly assigned probe branch. The contribution statements are used in analog procedural blocks along with other procedural statements.

Direct Contribution Statements

The direct contribution statements consist of a left-hand and a right-hand side, separated by a branch contribution punctuator <+:

nature-access-function (*branch-reference*) <+ *expression* ;
potential (*branch-reference*) <+ *expression* ;
flow (*branch-reference*) <+ *expression* ;

125

The left-hand side of the direct contribution statement provides access to the assigned branch signal using a signal access function. The right-hand side can be any expression that evaluates a numerical real value contributed to the branch signal. The *branch-reference* can be a named, unnamed, and hierarchical branch reference as described in the previous section. The only exception is a port branch reference that cannot be used in contribution statements.

The following examples demonstrate the application of the direct contribution statement in the conductor module:

```
module conductor(p, n);
    inout p, n;
    electrical p, n;
    branch (p,n) path;
    parameter real cond = 0;

    analog
        I(path) <+ cond * V(path);
endmodule
```

The use of direct contribution statements with local and hierarchical named and unnamed branch references, as well as a combination of local and hierarchical branch terminals, is demonstrated in the sources module:

```
module sources();
    electrical m;
    parameter real vref = 0.0;

    analog begin
      V(m) <+ vref;
      I(top.drv.br) <+ 1m;
```

```
    V(top.drv.branch(x,y)) <+ 1.2;
    V(m, top.drv.y) <+ 0.9;
  end
endmodule
```

Here, `br` is the branch, while `x` and `y` are nets declared in the `drv` module instance under the `top` module.

An important feature of direct contribution statements is that the value of the target may be expressed in terms of itself. This is referred to as an implicit or fixed-point formulation of the direct contribution statement. For example, in the contribution statement:

```
I(diode) <+ is*(exp((V(diode)-r*I(diode))/$vt)-1);
```

the signal access function `I(diode)` is found on both sides of the contribution statement. An alternative way to contribute branch signals implicitly is to use indirect contribution statements.

Indirect Contribution Statements

Indirect contribution statements allow the assignment of branch signal values in terms of implicit equations. It consists of a left-hand and a right-hand side, separated by a colon (`:`) punctuator:

```
nature-access-function ( branch-reference ) :  equation  ;
potential ( branch-reference ) :  equation  ;
flow ( branch-reference ) :  equation  ;
```

As in the direct contribution statements, the left-hand side provides assigned branch signal using a signal access function. The right-hand side specifies an equation defining the assigned signal value.

The basic syntax for the equations in indirect contribution statements is

```
nature-access-name ( branch-reference ) ==  expression
potential ( branch-reference ) ==  expression
flow ( branch-reference ) ==  expression
```

where the double equality punctuator (==) separates the left- and right-hand sides of the equation. The left-hand side of the equation is again a branch signal defined by the signal access function. However, it can be different than the assigned branch signal. On the right-hand side of the equation is an expression that evaluates a numerical real value. It can depend on the equation's left-hand side signal value.

Indirect contribution statements are incompatible with direct contribution statements across the same branch terminals. Once a value is indirectly assigned to a branch, it cannot be contributed to using the branch contribution operator <+. Hierarchical contributions are not allowed to branches that have been indirectly contributed. Indirect branch contributions shall not be used in looping and conditional statements unless the conditional expression is constant.

As an example, consider the use of indirect contribution in the module opamp representing a model of an ideal operational amplifier:

```
module opamp(out, pin, nin);
    inout out, pin, nin;
    electrical out, pin, nin;

    analog V(out) : V(pin, nin) == 0;

endmodule
```

The meaning of the indirect contribution here is to adjust the V(out) signal value so that the V(in) has zero value. It is equivalent to the implicit direct contribution statement:

```
V(out) <+ V(out) + V(pin, nin);
```

As another example, the direct implicit contribution to I(diode) can be expressed as an indirect contribution:

```
V(diode):
    I(diode) == is*(exp((V(diode)-r*I(diode))/$vt)-1);
```

The left-hand side of the equation in indirect contribution statements can be also a derivative or integral operator applied to a signal access function, which will be discussed in the next chapter.

Probe Branches

If branch potential or flow signal values are accessed in expressions with a signal access function but neither potential nor flow of that branch is contributed, the branch is considered to be a probe branch. The value of the probe branch signal which is not accessed by the signal access function is implicitly set to 0. If the probe branch flow value is accessed in an expression, the probe branch potential value is forced to 0. Otherwise, the branch flow value is forced to be 0 and the branch potential is available for use in an expression. Figure 8-4 shows a schematic representation of the potential and flow probe branches.

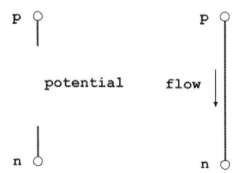

Figure 8-4. *Potential and flow probe branches*

The potential and flow of a probe branch may not both appear in expressions in a given module.

The following module defines a current-controlled current source:

```
module cccs (p, n, ps, ns);
    inout p, n, ps, ns;
    electrical p, n, ps, ns;
    parameter real A = 1.0;

    analog begin
        I(p,n) <+ A * I(ps,ns);
    end
endmodule
```

Because the branch flow I(ps,ns) appears in an expression on the right-hand side but neither its flow nor potential is contributed, it is a probe branch and its potential is implicitly assigned to 0.

Value Retention

Multiple direct contributions to the same branch are additive as shown in the following example of the amplifier module:

```
module amplifier (in, out);
    input in,
    output out;
    electrical in, out;
    parameter real gain = 1.0e3, rout = 1.0;

    analog begin
        // gain of amplifier
        V(out) <+ gain * V(in);
```

```
    // output resistance
    V(out) <+ rout * I(out);
end
```

```
endmodule
```

The value of the first contribution to the unnamed branch between the port out and ground is retained and the second contribution value is added to that retained value. The two contribution statements in the amplifier module have the same effect as a single contribution statement:

```
V(out) <+ gain * V(in) + rout * I(out);
```

Unlike variables, contributed values of branch signals are only valid for the current iteration. At the beginning of each iteration, the retained values of the branches used in direct contribution statements are reset to 0.

Contributing a flow to a branch that already has a value retained for the potential results in the potential being discarded and the branch being converted to a flow branch. Conversely, contributing a potential to a branch that already has a value retained for the flow results in the flow being discarded and the branch being converted into a potential branch:

```
module value_ret(p, n);
    inout p, n;
    electrical p, n;

    analog begin
      // no previously-retained value, 1 is retained
      V(p,n) <+ 1.0;

      // potential discarded; flow of 2 retained
      I(p,n) <+ 2.0;

      // flow discarded; potential of 3 retained
      V(p,n) <+ 3.0;
```

```
    // 4 added to previously-retained 3
    V(p,n) <+ 4.0;
  end
endmodule
```

The value retention rules specify that the preceding example will result in an assignment of 7.0 to the potential signal of the unnamed branch between ports p and n.

Switch Branches

Contribution to a branch may be switched between a potential and a flow during a simulation. To this end, contribution statements are allowed within conditional statements as shown in the example:

```
module relay (p, n, ps, pn);
   inout ps, ns;
   output p, n;
   electrical p, n;

   parameter real thresh=0;
   parameter real ron=0 from [0:inf);
   parameter real goff=0 from [0:1/ron);

   analog
      if (V(ps,ns) > thresh)
          V(p,n) <+ ron * I(p,n);
      else
          I(p,n) <+ goff * V(p,n);

endmodule
```

Using the switch branch between ports p and n, the module `relay` could represent also an ideal relay having zero on-resistance and zero off-conductance, set here as default.

The signals are contributed to switch branches using value retention rules. However, the switch branch expressions shall not use analog operators if the condition can change during a simulation. A discontinuity in the first derivative of signal values is implicitly assumed to occur when the branch switches and it is not necessary to explicitly announce it with the `$discontinuity` system task. The use of the `$discontinuity` system task is described in Chapter 16.

If a conditional contributed statement branch is not executed for any particular iteration, and it is not a probe branch, it shall be treated as a flow branch with a value of 0. For example, the conditional contribution:

```
if (closed)
    V(p,n) <+ 0;
```

is equivalent to

```
if (closed)
    V(p,n) <+ 0;
else
    I(p,n) <+ 0;
```

Conversely, if a flow is contributed to a branch in some iterations (when the condition is satisfied), and in other iterations, nothing is contributed, the branch is considered a potential branch with a value of 0.

In the following example of a `resistor` module, a switch branch is controlled with the runtime constant condition:

```
module resistor(a, b);
    inout a, b;
    electrical a, b;
    parameter real r = 1.0 from (0:inf);
```

```
analog begin
    if (r / $mfactor < 1.0e-3)
        V(a,b) <+ 0.0;
    else
        I(a,b) <+ V(a,b) / r;
end
endmodule
```

The switch branch is not switching during iterations. It will be either a potential or a flow branch based on the value of the effective resistance r/$mfactor evaluated in the elaboration phase. In the case that the voltage branch is selected, the resistance is simply shorted out, and the simulator may collapse the node to reduce the size of the system of equations.

CHAPTER 9

Derivative and Integral Operators

The branch potential and flow signals represent the system state space in the Verilog-A behavioral models. The state of a system is defined at every moment in time by a finite number of equations involving not only algebraic relationships of signal values but also differentiation and integration operations on the instantaneous values of the branch signals. To this end, Verilog-A provides time derivative and integral operators which can be used in procedural expressions. There is also a special application of time derivative and integral operators in indirect contribution equations. The additional probe derivative operator allows to access the first-order partial derivatives of any expression in the model with respect to branch signals.

Time Derivative Operator

The syntax of the time derivative operator takes one of the following forms:

```
ddt ( expression )
ddt ( expression, abstol )
ddt ( expression, nature-name )
```

The ddt() operator computes the time derivative of the *expression* argument. At the beginning of a transient simulation and in static analyses, ddt() returns zero.

An optional argument could be used to specify the absolute tolerance if needed. It is specified either as a constant expression or providing the nature identifier where the absolute tolerance is defined. Whether an absolute tolerance is needed depends on the context in which the ddt() operator is used. The absolute tolerance, defined by a constant expression or derived from the nature definition, represents the largest signal level considered negligible. The following branch contribution statement defines the linear capacitor and inductor using the time derivative operator:

```
I(p, n) <+ C * ddt(V(p, n), 1e-6);
V(p, n) <+ L * ddt(I(p, n), Current);
```

using the real literal and the nature name to define the optional *abstol* values in the ddt() operator.

Case Study: DC Motor

The DC motor converts electrical power to mechanical power of kinematic rotation. Figure 9-1 shows the schematic representation of the DC motor.

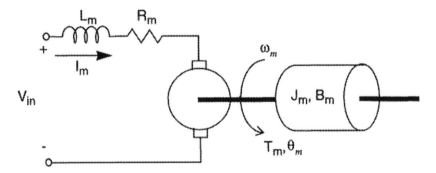

Figure 9-1. *Schematic representation of the DC motor*

The DC motor is described in simple terms by the following constitutive relations:

$$T_m = K_t I_m - B_m \theta_m - \frac{d}{dt}(J_m \theta_m)$$

$$V_{in} = R_m I_m + \frac{d}{dt}(L_m I_m) + K_m \theta_m$$

The electrical parameters of the motor model include its resistance R_m and inductance L_m. The mechanical parameters are motor inertia J_m and rotational friction B_m. The intrinsic motor voltage drop is K_m times the angular frequency of the motor θ_m, and the torque is K_t times the current through the motor, I_m. These equations are implemented in the Verilog-A model given in the motor_ckt module.

```
module motor(vp, vn, shaft);
    inout vp, vn, shaft;
    electrical vp, vn;
    rotational shaft;

    parameter real Km = 4.5, Kt = 6.2;
    parameter real j = 0.004, D = 0.1;
    parameter real Rm = 5.0, Lm = 0.02;

    analog begin
        V(vp, vn) <+ Km*Theta(shaft) + Rm*I(vp, vn) +
                    ddt(Lm*I(vp, vn), vp.flow.abstol);
        Tau(shaft) <+ Kt*I(vp, vn) - D*Theta(shaft) -
                    ddt(j*Theta(shaft), Angle);
    end
endmodule
```

Note the use of the hierarchical reference `vp.flow.abstol` to specify an absolute tolerance value for the `ddt()` operator. This syntax shall not be used for attributes whose value is not a constant expression.

Time Integrator Operator

The `idt()` operator computes the time integral of an expression. It can be used in one of the following syntax forms:

```
idt ( expression )
idt ( expression, ic )
idt ( expression, ic , assert )
idt ( expression, ic , assert , abstol )
idt ( expression, ic , assert , nature )
```

If only the *expression* argument is specified, the initial condition for the `idt()` operator is found by the simulator, generally, using the DC operating point preceding the transient simulation. However, for the DC operating point to exist, the `idt()` operator must be contained within a negative feedback loop that forces *expression* to 0. Otherwise, the output of the `idt()` operator is undefined.

The output of the integration operator can be forced to a particular value at the start of the transient simulation by specifying the initial condition *ic*. The optional numerical argument *assert* allows postponing the start of the integration and resetting the integration to the *ic* value. When specified with initial conditions (*ic*) but without *assert*, `idt()` returns the value of the initial condition on the initial point of a transient analysis. When specified with both initial conditions *ic* and *assert*, `idt()` returns the initial condition in DC (or other static) analyses, and whenever assert is nonzero. Once assert becomes zero, `idt()` returns the integral of the *expression* starting from the last instant where assert was nonzero.

The last optional parameter *abstol* or *nature* is used, similar to the ddt() operator, to specify an absolute tolerance if needed. Whether an absolute tolerance is needed depends on the context where idt() is used. The absolute tolerance applies to the input of the idt() operator and is the largest signal level considered negligible.

Case Study: Chemical Reaction System

The inflation of airbags, once the capsule has been ignited, is commonly described by the three concurrent chemical reactions:

$$2NaN_3 \rightarrow 2Na + 3N_2$$

$$10Na + 2KNO_3 \rightarrow K_2O + 5Na_2O + N_2$$

$$K_2O + Na_2O + SiO_2 \rightarrow K_2Na_2SiO_4$$

The chemical reaction equations can be rewritten to introduce the necessary time parameter. Using the Van't Hoff theory on kinetic equations results in the following set of reaction rate equations of chemical products over time:

$$\frac{d[NaN_3]}{dt} = -2k_1 [NaN_3]^2$$

$$\frac{d[Na]}{dt} = 2k_1 [NaN_3]^2 - 10k_2 *[Na]^{10}$$

$$\frac{d[N_2]}{dt} = 3k_1 [NaN_3]^2 + k_2 [Na]^{10} [KNO_3]^2$$

$$\frac{d[KNO_3]}{dt} = -2k_2[Na]^{10}[KNO_3]^2$$

$$\frac{d[K_2O]}{dt} = k_2[Na]^{10}[KNO_3]^2$$

$$\frac{d[Na_2O]}{dt} = 5k_2[Na]^{10}[KNO_3]^2 - k_3[K_2O][Na_2O][SiO_2]$$

$$\frac{d[SiO_2]}{dt} = -k_3[K_2O][Na_2O][SiO_2]$$

$$\frac{d[K_2Na_2SiO_4]}{dt} = k_3[K_2O][Na_2O][SiO_2]$$

where k_1 to k_3 represent reaction rate constants. The Verilog-A implementation of the chemical reaction model is shown in the chemsys module.

```
module chemsys (in);

    input electrical in;

    parameter real K1 = 14000.0;
    parameter real K2 = 1.0;
    parameter real K3 = 1.0;

    parameter thresh = 0.1;
    integer detain;

    chemical_sf c_NaN3, c_Na, c_N2, c_KNO3,
                c_K2O, c_Na2O, c_SiO2, c_K2Na2SiO4;

    analog initial detain = 1;
```

```
analog begin

   @(cross(V(in) - thresh, +1)) detain = 0

   CH(c_NaN3) <+ idt(-2.0*K1*pow(CH(c_NaN3),2),
                     5.0/3.0, detain);
   CH(c_Na)    <+ idt(2.0*K1*
                     pow(CH(c_NaN3),2)-10.0*K2*
                     pow(CH(c_Na),10)*
                     pow(CH(c_KNO3),2),
                     0.0, detain);
   CH(c_N2)    <+ idt(3.0*K1*pow(CH(c_NaN3),2) +
                     K2*pow(CH(c_Na),10)*
                     pow(CH(c_KNO3),2),
                     0.0, detain);
   CH(c_KNO3) <+ idt(-2.0*K2*pow(CH(c_Na),10)*
                     pow(CH(c_KNO3),2),
                     1.0/3.0, detain);
   CH(c_K2O)   <+ idt(K2*pow(CH(c_Na),10)*
                     pow(CH(c_KNO3),2)-
                     K3*CH(c_K2O)*
                     CH(c_Na2O)*CH(c_SiO2),
                     0.0, detain);
   CH(c_Na2O) <+ idt(5.0*K2*pow(CH(c_Na),10)*
                     pow(CH(c_KNO3),2)-
                     K3*CH(c_K2O)*
                     CH(c_Na2O)*CH(c_SiO2),
                     0.0, detain);
   CH(c_SiO2) <+ idt(-K3*CH(c_K2O)*
                     CH(c_Na2O)*CH(c_SiO2),
                     1.0/6.0, detain);
```

141

```
CH(c_K2Na2SiO4) <+ idt(K3*CH(c_K2O)*
                         CH(c_Na2O)*CH(c_SiO2),
                         0.0, detain);
    end

endmodule  // chemsys
```

The equations of the chemical system are implemented in its integral form using the idt() operator. This form is preferred since it provides a way to postpone the integration of equations until it is triggered by external signals. It is handled by the *assert* argument to the idt() operator, which is in the module implementation provided by the integer variable detain.

Circular Integrator Operator

The idtmod() operator converts an expression argument into its indefinitely integrated value similar to the idt() operator. The idtmod() operator can be used in one of the syntax forms:

```
idtmod ( expression )
idtmod ( expression , ic )
idtmod ( expression , ic ,modulus )
idtmod ( expression , ic ,modulus, offset )
idtmod ( expression , ic ,modulus, offset , const-expr )
idtmod ( expression , ic , modulus, offset, nature )
```

The initial condition *ic* is used in the same way as in the idt() operator. If idtmod() is used in a system with a feedback configuration that forces *expression* to 0, the initial condition can be omitted without any unexpected behavior during simulation.

The return value of the idtmod() operator can be expressed as

$$y_{mod}(t) = y(t) - k \cdot m$$

where $y(t)$ is the return value of the time integrator operator idt(), m is the *modulus*, while k is an integer chosen so that the output shall remain in the range

$$b \le y(t) \le b + m$$

where b is the *offset*. The *modulus* and *offset* shall be expressions that evaluate real values and the value of the *modulus* shall be positive. If the *modulus* is not specified, then idtmod() shall behave like the idt() operator and not limit the output of the integrator. If the offset is not given, the default value of 0 is assumed.

Figure 9-2 shows an example of idtmod() operator output.

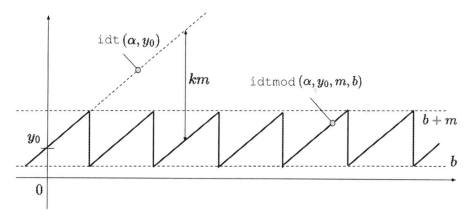

Figure 9-2. *The output of the idtmod() operator when the input argument is a constant α*

Besides keeping its output bounded, the idtmod() operator is implemented in such a way that its internal state variable is also bounded.

Case Study: Voltage-Controlled Oscillator

The circular integrator is particularly useful in cases where the time integral can get very large. A typical example of such a system is a voltage-controlled oscillator (VCO) shown in Figure 9-3.

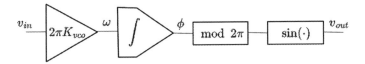

Figure 9-3. *Schematic representation of the voltage-controlled oscillator*

The VCO produces an output signal whose frequency is proportional to an input signal.

$$f_{out} = K_{vco} v_{in}(t)$$

where K_{vco} is the VCO gain. To achieve this functionality, it is required to integrate the input signal to compute the phase of the output signal:

$$\phi(t) = 2\pi K_{vco} \cdot \operatorname*{mod}_{2\pi} \left(\int_0^t v_{in}(\tau) d\tau - 0.5 \right) + 0.5$$

and then produce the output signal from the phase as

$$v_{out} = \sin(\phi(t))$$

The Verilog-A code that implements this model is given in the vco module:

```
module vco (out, in);
    input voltage in;
    output voltage out;
```

```
parameter real Vmin = 0;
parameter real Vmax = Vmin + 1 from (Vmin:inf);
parameter real Fmin = 1 from (0:inf);
parameter real Fmax = 2 * Fmin from (Fmin:inf);
parameter real ampl = 1; // output amplitude (V)

real freq, phase;

analog begin
   //compute the freq from the input voltage
   freq = (V(in) - Vmin)*(Fmax - Fmin) /
          (Vmax - Vmin) + Fmin;

   //phase is the integral of the freq modulo
   phase = 2*`M_PI*idtmod(freq, 0.0, 1.0, -0.5);

   //generate the output
   V(out) <+ sin(phase);
end
endmodule
```

In a VCO, only the output values in the range [0,2π] of the circular integrator are of interest. The file `constants.vams` supplies `M_PI` defined to be the Pi number. The use of the `constants.vams` file and compiler directives is explained in Chapter 20.

Indirect Contribution Equations

The Verilog-A syntax allows defining an indirect branch contribution with derivative and integral operator–based expressions on the equation's left-hand side:

derivative-or-integral-operator == *expression*

Here, *derivative-or-integral-operator* is obtained by applying a derivative or an integral operator to the branch signal access functions:

```
ddt( nature-access-function ( branch-reference ), ... )
idt( nature-access-function ( branch-reference ), ... )
idtmod( nature-access-function ( branch-reference ), ... )
```

with an optional argument specified if required.

The use of derivative and integral operators in indirect contribution statements is quite useful for the description of differential and integral equations. For example, the indirect contribution statements

```
Pos(velocity):ddt(Pos(y)) == Pos(velocity);
Pos(y):ddt(Pos(velocity)) == B*pow(Pos(y),3.0);
```

describe the nonlinear equation of motion.

For multiple indirect contribution statements, the targets frequently can be paired with any equation. For example, the following ordinary differential equation

$$\frac{dx}{dt} = f(x,y,z)$$

$$\frac{dy}{dt} = g(x,y,z)$$

$$\frac{dz}{dt} = h(x,y,z)$$

Where x, y, and z are electrical quantities, can be written as

```
V(x): ddt(V(x)) == f(V(x), V(y), V(z));
V(y): ddt(V(y)) == g(V(x), V(y), V(z));
V(z): ddt(V(z)) == h(V(x), V(y), V(z));
```

or

```
V(y): ddt(V(x)) == f(V(x), V(y), V(z));
V(z): ddt(V(y)) == g(V(x), V(y), V(z));
V(x): ddt(V(z)) == h(V(x), V(y), V(z));
```

or

```
V(z): ddt(V(x)) == f(V(x), V(y), V(z));
V(x): ddt(V(y)) == g(V(x), V(y), V(z));
V(y): ddt(V(z)) == h(V(x), V(y), V(z));
```

without affecting the results.

Case Study: Accelerometer

The accelerometer has the structure shown in Figure 9-4. Similar to the
DC motor example, it mixes mechanical and electrical disciplines in
two transducers. First, the input force is converted into a mechanical
displacement using a tethered seismic mass. Then, the mechanical
displacement is converted into an electrical signal by modulating the gap
between capacitance plates.

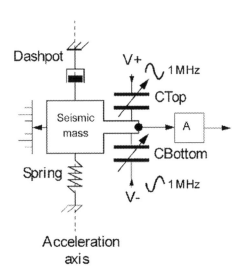

Figure 9-4. *Schematic representation of an accelerometer*

In the first transducer, the micro-flexural structure can be modeled as a damped harmonic oscillator using a second-order differential equation:

$$F(t) = M\frac{d^2x}{dt} + D\frac{dx}{dt} + kx$$

where $F(t)$ is the force applied to a seismic mass, x is the displacement of the mass M, D is the damping coefficient, and k is spring stiffness.

The second transducer uses the seismic mass as the middle plate of a differential capacitance circuit. The displacement of the seismic mass modifies the gap between plates and, hence, the differential capacitance values.

The Verilog-A code that implements this model is given in the capsensor module:

```
module capsensor (mass, etop, emid, ebot);
    inout mass, mref, etop, emid, ebot;
    kinematic mass;
    electrical etop, emid, ebot;
```

```
// mechanical properties
parameter real M  = 0.16e-9; // seismic mass
parameter real D  = 4.0e-6;  // damping coeff.
parameter real K  = 2.6455;  // spring stiffness
parameter real A  = 220.0e-12; // capacitor area
parameter real D0 = 1.5e-6; // initial position

real ctm, cbm, tmp;

analog begin
    // equation for displacement of comb drive
    tmp = F(mass)- K * Pos(mass);
    Pos(mass):
        ddt(Pos(mass))==(idt(tmp)-D*Pos(mass))/M;

    // compute change and current in capacitances
    ctm = A*`P_EPS0 / (D0 + Pos(mass));
    cbm = A*`P_EPS0 / (D0 - Pos(mass));
    I(etop, emid) <+ ctm * ddt(V(etop, emid));
    I(ebot, emid) <+ cbm * ddt(V(ebot, emid));

  end
endmodule
```

Note the use of the indirect contribution statement for the displacement of the seismic mass Pos(mass).

Probe Derivative Operator

The probe derivative operator provides access to symbolically computed partial derivatives of expressions in the analog procedural blocks. The syntax for the probe derivative operator is

```
ddx ( expression , unknown-quantity )
```

The first argument is the expression that evaluates a real numerical value. The ddx() operator returns the partial derivative of its first argument with respect to the second argument *unknown_quantity* which is the branch probe (potential or flow probe) keeping all other unknowns fixed and evaluated at the current operating point. If the *expression* does not depend explicitly on the *unknown-quantity*, then ddx() returns 0. Care must be taken when using implicit equations or indirect contributions, for which the simulator may create internal unknowns; derivatives to these internal unknowns cannot be accessed with ddx(). Unlike the ddt() operator, no tolerance specifications are required for the ddx() operator because the partial derivative is computed symbolically and evaluated at the current operating point.

In many cases, the values of derivatives of expressions used in contribution statements are useful quantities. It is particularly true for compact modeling where quantities such as the transconductance of a transistor or the capacitance of a nonlinear charge-storage element such as a varactor are essential for the circuit and system design.

The following example of a module diode uses a ddx() operator to obtain the conductance of the diode:

```
module diode(a,c);
    inout a, c;
    electrical a, c;
    parameter real IS = 1.0e-14;
    real idio;
    (* desc="small-signal conductance" *) real gdio;
    analog begin
        idio = IS * (limexp(V(a,c)/$vt) - 1);
        gdio = ddx(idio, V(a));
        I(a,c) <+ idio;
    end
endmodule
```

The variable gdio is declared as an output variable (using the attribute instance described in Chapter 19) so that its value is available for inspection by the designer.

The next example implements a voltage-controlled dependent current source and is used to illustrate the computations of partial derivatives:

```
module vccs(pout, nout, pin, nin);
    inout pout, nout, pin, nin;
    electrical pout, nout, pin, nin;
    parameter real k = 1.0;
    real vin, one, minusone, zero;

    analog begin
        vin = V(pin,nin);
        one = ddx(vin, V(pin));
        minusone = ddx(vin, V(nin));
        zero = ddx(vin, V(pout));
        I(pout,nout) <+ k * vin;
    end
endmodule
```

The names of the variables indicate the values of the partial derivatives: +1, –1, or 0.

CHAPTER 10

Built-In Math Functions

There are an infinite number of possible math functions. But in practice, there is a definite set of standard math functions that are considered reasonable to include as primitives in expressions and that are implemented as built-in math functions in Verilog-A. Besides the standard deterministic functions, Verilog-A also provides a set of probabilistic functions to support variability-aware system simulation.

Deterministic Functions

A function is considered deterministic if it always returns the same result when it's called with the same input arguments. It can be invoked using the traditional Verilog-A syntax style:

```
function-name (x)
function-name (x,y)
```

where the *function-name* is followed by parentheses specifying one or two function arguments. Alternatively, one can use a system function syntax style:

```
$function-name (x)
$function-name (x,y)
```

© Slobodan Mijalković 2022
S. Mijalković, *A Practical Guide to Verilog-A*, https://doi.org/10.1007/978-1-4842-6351-8_10

where the function name is preceded by the $ character. With just a few exceptions, most of the Verilog-A built-in math functions can be used in both syntax styles. Although the Verilog-A standard encourages if possible the adoption of the system function style, in this book the system function style is used only if the transitional Verilog-A function style is not possible.

Logarithmic and Power Functions

The logarithmic and power functions supported by Verilog-A are shown in Table 10-1. They are all available in both traditional Verilog-A and system function styles.

Table 10-1. *Power and logarithmic functions in Verilog-A*

Function Name	Verilog-A Function	Domain
Natural logarithm	$\ln(x)$	$x>0$
Decimal logarithm	$\log(x)$	$x>0$
Exponential	$\exp(x)$	All x
Square root	$\text{sqrt}(x)$	$x>=0$
Power	$\text{pow}(x,\ y)$	If $x>0$, all y If $x=0$, $y>0$ If $x<0$, int(y)
Hypot	$\text{hypot}(x,y)$	All x, all y

The $\ln(x)$ and $\log(x)$ return the natural and decimal logarithms of a real argument whose value must be positive. The $\exp(x)$ returns the exponential function value for a real argument x. The $\ln(x)$ is the inverse function of $\exp(x)$.

Note   Unlike the C programming language where the log(x) function is used to evaluate the natural logarithm, in Verilog-A the natural logarithm is evaluated using the ln(x) function, while the log(x) function evaluates decimal logarithms.

The sqrt(x) returns the square root function value for a non-negative real argument x. The pow(x, y) returns x raised to the power of y, which can be also achieved using expression x**y. The hypot(x,y) returns the square root of the sum of squares of its arguments, $\sqrt{x^2 + y^2}$. This corresponds to calculating the length of the hypotenuse of a right-angled triangle.

Trigonometric Functions

The trigonometric functions supported by Verilog-A are shown in Table 10-2. They are all available in both traditional Verilog-A and system function styles.

Table 10-2. *Trigonometric functions in Verilog-A*

Function Name	Verilog-A Function	Domain
Sine	sin(x)	All x
Cosine	cos(x)	All x
Tangent	tan(x)	x != n(π/2), n is odd
Arc-sine	asin(x)	-1<=x<=1
Arc-cosine	acos(x)	-1<=x<=1
Arc-tangent	atan(x)	All x
2-argument arc-tangent	atan2(x,y)	All x, all y atan2(0,0)=0

Arguments to the trigonometric functions (sin(), cos(), tan()) and return values of the inverse trigonometric functions (asin(), acos(), atan(), atan2()) are in radians. Input values outside of the valid range for the operator shall report an error.

The function atan2(x,y) is defined as the angle in the Euclidean plane, given in radians, between the positive y axis and the ray from the origin to the point (x, y). For $y>0$, atan2(x,y) = atan(x/y). However, for $y>0$ the single-argument arc-tangent function atan(x/y) cannot distinguish between diametrically opposite directions. In addition, an attempt to find the angle between the y axis and the vectors $(x, 0)$, $x \neq 0$ requires evaluation of arctan$(x/0)$, which fails on division by zero. The atan2() function calculates one unique arc-tangent value from two variables x and y, where the signs of both arguments are used to determine the quadrant of the result, thereby selecting the desired branch of the arc-tangent of x/y.

Hyperbolic Functions

The hyperbolic functions supported by Verilog-A are shown in Table 10-3. They are all available in both traditional Verilog-A and system function styles.

Table 10-3. *Hyperbolic functions in Verilog-A*

Function Name	Verilog-A Function	Domain
Hyperbolic sine	sinh(x)	All x
Hyperbolic cosine	cosh(x)	All x
Hyperbolic tangent	tanh(x)	All x
Arc-hyperbolic sine	asinh(x)	All x
Arc-hyperbolic cosine	acosh(x)	All x
Arc-hyperbolic tangent	atanh(x)	All x

Arguments to the hyperbolic functions ($sinh(x)$, $cosh(x)$, $tanh(x)$) and return values of the inverse hyperbolic functions ($asinh()$, $acosh()$, $atanh()$) are called a hyperbolic angle.

Limiting and Rounding Functions

A number of limiting and rounding functions supported in Verilog-A are shown in Table 10-4. Note that the $min()$, $max()$, and $abs()$ functions are not available in the system function style, while the $clog2()$ function can be used only in the system function syntax style.

Table 10-4. *Limiting and rounding functions in Verilog-A*

Function Name	Verilog-A Function	Domain
Minimum	$min(x, y)$	All x, all y
Maximum	$max(x, y)$	All x, all y
Absolute	$abs(x)$	All x
Floor	$floor(x)$	All x
Ceiling	$ceil(x)$	All x
Ceiling of log base 2	$clog2(x)$	All x

The $min(x,y)$ and $max(x,y)$ return the minimum or maximum of two integer or real numbers x and y. The $abs(x)$ function returns the absolute value of an argument x of type integer or real. These functions can be also implemented using the conditional operator:

$min(x,y)$ is equivalent to $(x < y)$? x : y

$max(x,y)$ is equivalent to $(x > y)$? x : y

$abs(x)$ is equivalent to $(x > 0)$? x : $-x$

For min(), max(), and abs() functions, the result is of type integer if arguments are of type integer and otherwise it is real. If either operand of min() and max() functions is real, both are converted to real, as is the result. Note that the min(), max(), and abs() functions have discontinuous derivatives. It is therefore necessary to define the behavior of the derivative of these functions at the point of the discontinuity.

The floor(x) function returns the greatest integer less than or equal to its real argument. On the other hand, the ceil(x) function returns the least integer greater than or equal to its real argument. These functions are piecewise constant and discontinuous.

The system function $clog2() shall return the ceiling of logarithm base 2 of the argument. The argument can be of integer or real type and an argument value of 0 shall produce a result of 0.

Probabilistic Functions

Verilog-A provides a function for random number generation and a set of statistical distribution functions. They can be only used in a system function syntax style.

Random Number Generation Function

The probabilistic function $arandom provides a mechanism for generating a sequence of random numbers. It is used in one of the syntax forms:

```
$arandom
$arandom ( seed )
$arandom ( seed , type-string )
```

The random number returned is a 32-bit signed integer that can be positive or negative. The $arandom functions return a new random integer number each time it is called.

The *seed* is an optional argument that determines the sequence of random numbers generated. The same sequence of random numbers will be generated every time the same *seed* is used. It could be important for regression analysis where each simulation run must work with the same sequence of random numbers. The $arandom function could be called by the function name only, in which case the simulator picks a seed.

The *seed* may be specified as an integer variable, integer parameter, or integer constant. If the *seed* is specified as an integer variable, it is a bidirectional argument; that is, a value is passed to the function and a different value is returned. The variable should be initialized prior to calling $arandom and only updated by the $arandom function. If the *seed* is specified as an integer parameter or an integer constant, the $arandom function does not update the seed value. However, an internal seed is created which is assigned the initial value of the parameter or constant. The internal seed gets updated every time the call to $arandom is made. This allows the $arandom function to be used for parameter initialization. In order to get different random values when the *seed* argument is an integer parameter, the user can override the parameter value.

The *type-string* is an additional optional argument of a string type. It provides support for Monte-Carlo analysis and shall only be used in calls to $arandom from within a paramset. If the *type-string* is "global" (or not specified in a call within a paramset), then one value is generated for each Monte-Carlo trial. If the *type-string* is "instance", then one value is generated for each instance that references this value, and a new set of values for these instances is generated for each Monte-Carlo trial.

For example, the following code fragment:

```
integer rand;
rand = $arandom % 60;
```

assigns a random number between -59 and 59 to the rand variable.

Statistical Distribution Functions

Verilog-A provides a number of statistical distribution functions which are invoked using a generic system function syntax form:

$rdist_*distribution-function-name*(arg, ...)

where *distribution-function-name* stands for different distribution function names given in Table 10-5.

Table 10-5. *Statistical distribution functions in Verilog-A*

Name	Argument List
chi_square	*seed, mean*
	seed, mean, type-string
exponential	*seed, mean*
	seed, mean, type-string
poisson	*seed, mean*
	seed, mean, type-string
uniform	*seed, start, end*
	seed, start, end, type-string
erlang	*seed, k-stage, mean*
	seed, k-stage, mean, type-string
normal	*seed, mean, standard-dev*
	seed, mean, standard-dev, type-string
t	*seed, degree-of-freedom*
	seed, degree-of-freedom, type-string

Each of these functions returns a random number whose characteristics are described by the function name. For example, $rdist_uniform returns random numbers uniformly distributed in the interval specified by its arguments. All probabilistic functions return a real value. All arguments to the probabilistic functions are real values, except for the *seed* which shall be an integer value. Moreover, the arguments *mean*, *degree-of-freedom*, and *k-stage* shall be greater than zero. Otherwise, an error shall be reported.

The *mean* argument causes the average value returned by the statistical distribution function to approach the specified value by the *mean* argument.

In $rdist_uniform, the *start* and *end* arguments are input arguments that bound the returned function values. The *start* value shall be smaller than the *end* value.

The *standard-dev* argument, used by $rdist_normal, is an input argument that helps to determine the shape of the density function. Using larger numbers for *standard-dev* spreads the returned values over a wider range of values. Using a *mean* of 0 and a *standard-dev* of 1, the $rdist_ normal function generates the Gaussian distribution.

The *degree-of-freedom* argument helps determine the shape of the density function. Using larger numbers for *degree-of-freedom* spreads the returned values over a wider value range.

The use of the *seed* argument is the same as for the $arandom function. The statistical distribution functions shall always return the same value given the same seed. This facilitates debugging by making the operation of the system repeatable. In order to get different random values when the seed argument is a parameter, the user can override the parameter.

The use of the *type-string* arguments in statistical distribution functions is the same as in the $arandom function. It provides support for Monte-Carlo analysis and shall only be used in calls to a distribution function from within a paramset. If the *type-string* is "global" (or not specified in a call within a paramset), then one value is generated for each Monte-Carlo trial. If the *type-string* is "instance", then one value is generated for each instance that references this value, and a new set of values for these instances is generated for each Monte-Carlo trial.

The following example shows how to use the $rdist_normal function to model two kinds of statistical variation:

```
module semicoCMOS ();
    localparam real tox = 3e-8;
    localparam real dtox_g =
                    $rdist_normal(1,0,1n,"global");
    localparam real dtox_mm =
                    $rdist_normal(2,0,5n,"instance");
endmodule

paramset nch nmos3; // mismatch paramset
    parameter real l=1u from [0.25u:inf);
    parameter real w=1u from [0.2u:inf);
    parameter integer mm=0 from (0:1];
    .l=l; .w=w; .ad=w*0.5u; .as=w*0.5u;
    .kp=5e-5; .u0=650; .nsub=1.3e17;
    .vmax=0; .tpg=1; .nfs=0.8e12;
    .tox = semicoCMOS.tox + semicoCMOS.dtox_g +
            semicoCMOS.dtox_mm;
endparamset

module top ();
    electrical d1, d2, g, vdd, gnd;
    ground gnd; nch #(.l(1u), .w(5u), .mm(1))
    m1(.d(d1), .g(g), .s(gnd), .b(gnd));
    nch #(.l(1u), .w(5u), .mm(1))
        m2(.d(d2), .g(g), .s(gnd), .b(gnd));
    resistor #(.r(1k)) R1 (vdd, d1);
    resistor #(.r(1k)) R2 (vdd, d2);
    vsine #(.dc(2.5)) Vdd (vdd, gnd);
    vsine #(.dc(0), .ampl(1.0), .offset(1.5),
            .freq(1k)) Vg (g, gnd);
endmodule
```

Because the local parameter dtox_mm is obtained from $rdist_normal with the string "instance", the instances m1 and m2 will get different values of tox. Though the local variation has a smaller standard deviation than the global variation, only the local variation will affect the differential voltage between nodes d1 and d2.

CHAPTER 11

User-Defined Functions

Besides the predefined math functions, described in the previous chapter, Verilog-A provides also a way to define our own functions. User-defined functions could be used to encapsulate self-contained segments of the code and avoid the replication of the same or very similar code sections. Moreover, testing can be carried out on each function in isolation, rather than on the whole module. This chapter describes the two main stages in using the user-defined functions, first how to define a function and second how to invoke it in the module procedural code.

Defining Functions

User functions are defined between the keywords `function` and `endfunction` using the syntax

```
analog function function-type function-name ;
  declaration-statement ...
  procedural-statement
endfunction
```

The function definition must be preceded by the keyword `analog` to distinguish it from digital style function definitions in the Verilog-AMS language using Verilog-A as a language subset. The header line, ending

© Slobodan Mijalković 2022
S. Mijalković, *A Practical Guide to Verilog-A*, https://doi.org/10.1007/978-1-4842-6351-8_11

with a semicolon, declares a function type as *function-type* and a function name as an identifier *function-name*. The *function-type* can be either `real` or `integer` but the declaration of the function type is optional. If the function type is not specified, it is assumed to be `real`. The user-defined functions can be only defined within a module body along with other two analog constructs, namely, `analog` blocks and `analog initial` blocks. It is not allowed to position the function definition within procedural blocks.

The body of the user-defined function definition consists of a sequence of declaration statements followed by a single procedural statement. The syntax allows the declaration of real and integer variables and parameters but the declaration of nets is not permitted. The declared variables and parameters have only local scope within a user-defined function. Some of the declared variables shall be specified as formal arguments to provide an interface for calling user-defined functions in the module procedural code.

Formal Arguments

A user-defined function shall have at least one variable specified as a formal argument. The syntax for the specification of scalar formal arguments is

```
direction variable-name,  ...
```

The *direction* specifier can be either an `input` or `output` keyword for unidirectional or an `inout` keyword for bidirectional formal arguments. The direction specifier is followed by a comma-separated list of variable names. The declaration of formal arguments with the `direction` specifier resembles the port declarations but here variable names are used instead of port names. Besides, all formal arguments shall be also declared as integer or real variables:

```
input l, w;
output area, perim;
real l, w, area, perim;
```

Array variables can be also specified as formal arguments using the syntax:

```
direction range port-name,  ...
```

where a range specifier is introduced after the direction specifier, similar to the declarations of the vector ports:

```
inout [0:1]a;
real a[0:1];
```

The ranges in the direction and type declarations must be identical.

If a formal argument only receives values from outside of the function, it is specified as an input argument. The modification done to the input arguments in the function evaluation does not reflect in the caller's scope.

An argument does not have to receive anything from outside of the function. It can be used to pass a computation result back to the outside world. In this case, it is specified as an output argument. All output arguments are implicitly initialized to 0.

Finally, an argument can receive a value, use it for computation, and hold a result so that it can be passed back to the outside world. In this case, it is specified as an inout argument. The modification done on inout arguments in the function evaluation is persistent and changes are reflected in the caller's scope. The inout arguments do not get initialized to 0 like output arguments.

A Return Variable

The user-defined functions implicitly declare an additional variable with local function scope. It has the same type and name as the function itself. This local implicit variable is initialized to 0 and can be assigned within the body of the user-defined function. It is illegal to declare another variable with the same name inside the user-defined function scope. For example, in the user-defined function:

```
analog function real hypsmooth;
    input x, c;
    real x, c;

    hypsmooth = 0.5 * (x + hypot(x, 2c));
endfunction
```

the hypsmooth is implicitly declared a return variable of type real. The last value assigned to this variable will be the return value of the user-defined function. If this internal variable is not assigned during the execution of the user-defined function, then the user-defined function will return the initialized value of 0. A user-defined function shall always return a scalar numerical value.

A Procedural Statement

A single procedural statement in user-defined functions could be a procedural assignment (as in the previous example of the hypsmooth function), but also any statements available for conditional execution, or a single sequential block statement. Named block statements, and corresponding block declarations, are not allowed in user-defined functions.

The procedural statement actually evaluates the user-defined function. It should only reference locally defined variables (including formal arguments), locally defined parameters, but also module-level parameters. If a locally defined parameter with the specified name does not exist, then the module-level parameter of the specified name will be used. Since it is not possible to declare and reference nets within user-defined functions, access functions and analog operators are not allowed in the procedural statement. The event control statements are not allowed, too.

The following example illustrates a user-defined function using scalar and array arguments. The maxValue function

```
analog function real maxValue;
    input n1, n2;
    real n1, n2;

    maxValue = (n1 > n2) ? n1 : n2;
endfunction
```

returns the larger value of two input arguments. The distance function

```
analog function real distance;
    input [0:2] p;
    input [0:2] q;
    real p[0:2], q[0:2];

    distance = sqrt( (p[0]-q[0])**2 +
                     (p[1]-q[1])**2 +
                     (p[2]-q[2])**2 );
endfunction
```

returns the distance between two points in space. The geomcalc function

```
analog function real geomcalc;
    input l, w;
    output area, perim;
    real area, w, l, perim;
    begin
        area = l * w;
        perim = 2 * ( l + w );
    end
endfunction
```

evaluates the area and perimeter of a rectangle as output arguments. Finally, the arrayadd function

```
analog function real arrayadd;
    inout [0:1]a;
    input [0:1]b;
    real a[0:1], b[0:1];
    integer i;
    begin
        for(i = 0; i < 2; i = i + 1) begin
            a[i] = a[i] + b[i];
        end
    end
endfunction
```

adds the contents of a second array argument to the first one.

Calling Functions

The user-defined function shall only be called from an analog block or from within another user-defined function. They shall not call themselves directly or indirectly, which means that recursive functions are not permitted.

The user-defined function is typically called in two styles: as an operand in expressions or as a stand-alone statement similar to subroutines or procedures in programming languages. Both styles are using the same function reference syntax but could select different ways of exchanging data by calling procedural code.

Function References

A function call operator with the syntax

function-name (*expression*, ...)

is used as a user-defined function reference in the module procedural code. It specifies the list of expressions in parentheses after the user-defined function name. These expressions represent actual arguments of the function reference. During the execution of a user-defined function, the appropriate linkage must be established between the actual arguments, specified in the function call operator, and the formal arguments defined within the function. This linkage is called argument association.

The argument association in user-defined functions is based on the order in which the direction of the formal arguments is specified in the function definition. For example, the function reference

```
geomcalc(l-dl, w-dw, ar, per);
```

supplies the actual arguments in the order in which the formal argument directions are specified in the user-defined function geomcalc:

```
analog function real geomcalc;
    input l, w;
    output area, perim;
    real area, w, l, perim;
    ...
  endfunction
```

Here, it is associating l-dl with l, w-dw with w, ar with area, and per with perim. Note that the order of arguments in their type declarations is not relevant at all for the argument association. The order of evaluation of actual argument expressions in the function reference is undefined.

Using Functions in Expressions

One way a user-defined function may be referenced or invoked in module procedural code is by placing the function reference with actual arguments as an operand in an expression. In that case, a user-defined function is typically defined to have only input arguments. The result of the function evaluation shall be assigned to the implicitly declared return variable.

Here are examples of using user-defined functions maxValue, hypsmooth, and distance in expressions:

```
V(out) <+ maxValue(V(in1), V(in2));
Vdsat = hypsmooth(Vdsat-1.0E-3, 1.0E-5) + 1.0E-3;
vel = distance('{x1, y1, z1},'{x2, y2, z2})) / time;
```

Any expression that evaluates a numerical value, including signal access functions, can be used here as actual function arguments. Note the use of assignment patterns to match up the formal array arguments in the function distance.

Function Called As Statements

The user-defined functions are called in a statement style if it is intended to return more than one value from the function. In that case, the implicitly defined return variable is not used. Instead, output and inout arguments are used to return the values evaluated by the user-defined function.

During the execution of the function, inout and output arguments can be assigned in the procedural statement. At the end of the function execution, the last value assigned to the inout and output arguments is assigned to the corresponding variable reference that was passed into the function. If a value was not assigned to an inout argument during the execution of the analog user-defined function, then the corresponding actual argument reference is left untouched. If a value was not assigned to an output argument, the corresponding actual argument will be reset to 0, the initial value of output arguments.

Note   *inout* arguments are not "pass by reference" as it is in the C programming language, but more closely related to "copy in" and "copy out." Care should be taken to avoid passing the same variable to different *inout* and *output* arguments of the same user-defined function as the results are undefined.

The argument passed to an inout or output argument must be a variable reference. As an example, consider the call to geomcalc in the statement style as

```
dummy = geomcalc(l-dl, w-dw, ar, per);
```

The first two actual arguments are expressions and match up with the input specification of the l and w formal arguments. However, the other two arguments must be real identifiers because they should associate with the output formal arguments area and perim. The statement

```
dummy = geomcalc(l-dl, w-dw, ar/2, V(a));
```

incorrectly uses the geomcalc function since the third argument is passed an expression and the fourth argument is passed the potential probe V(a), both not the variable reference, and it will result in a compilation error.

Note that the function reference cannot represent the statement itself. It is still an expression and the statement is artificially created by assigning the return function value to a *dummy* variable.

If the inout or output argument is defined as an array, then the argument passed into the function must be an array variable or an array assignment pattern of the equivalent size. The following example demonstrates passing array arguments to the arrayadd user-defined function:

```
x[0] = 5; x[1] = 10;
y = 3; z = 6;
dummy = arrayadd(x,'{y,z});
```

Here, the first and second arguments are both expecting arrays. An array variable name x is passed for the first argument and an array assignment pattern of two scalar variables has been used for the second argument. Since the first argument is an inout argument, the result of calling the arrayinit function will update the vector variable x with values x[0] = 8 and x[1] = 16.

CHAPTER 12

Lookup Tables

A Verilog-A procedural block could be in principle interpreted as a multivariate input-output mapping. It takes a set of parameters, variables, or expressions at the input, for producing certain results at the end of the procedural evaluation sequence. In some cases, the analytical model for such procedural evaluation could be unavailable or too time-consuming for implementation. One way to overcome this problem is to implement such critical input-output procedural mappings in Verilog-A code using lookup tables. The savings in processing time can be significant because retrieving a value from a data table is often much faster than carrying out expensive input-output procedural computations.

Table Data Structure

The lookup table data are commonly generated by data acquisition systems or precalculated by detailed simulations. Care must be taken when preparing the table data. The Verilog-A LUT model function requires a specific data format, and incorrectly formatted tables can cause errors in calling the function. Worse yet, misaligned or improperly formatted data could be interpreted incorrectly, causing subtle errors in the simulation results.

© Slobodan Mijalković 2022
S. Mijalković, *A Practical Guide to Verilog-A*, https://doi.org/10.1007/978-1-4842-6351-8_12

Jagged Array Grids

A lookup table is basically an indexed multidimensional array of input-output data values. The simplest and commonly used LUT array data structure is a rectangular multidimensional array or grid. It is convenient to represent the rectangular grids as a nested set of 1-D arrays, or a recursively introduced array of arrays:

$$\left\{ x_{i_1}^{(1)}, i_1 = 1, N^{(1)} \left\{ x_{i_2}^{(2)}, i_2 = 1, N^{(2)} \ldots \left\{ x_{i_d}^{(d)}, i_d = 1, N^{(d)} \right\} \right\} \right\}$$

Here, $N^{(i)}$ is the number of grid points with respect to the ith array dimension. The data structure of nested 1-D arrays is also compatible with commonly used parametric sweeping schemes in analog simulators and data acquisition systems which can be used to sample LUT data. However, the simplicity of rectangular grid LUTs does not come without a price. Namely, the total number of grid data points

$$N = \prod_{i=1}^{d} N^{(i)}$$

grows exponentially with the table dimension. The grid-based LUTs obviously underlie the curse of dimensionality and thus in practice they are almost never used for $d > 3$.

The curse of dimensionality could be effectively overcome with Verilog-A LUT models based on jagged (also called ragged) arrays, or jagged grids. Similar to a multidimensional array, a jagged array is also recursively defined as an array of arrays:

$$\left\{ x_{i_1}^{(1)}, i_1 = 1, N^{(1)} \left\{ x_{(i_1)i_2}^{(2)}, i_2 = 1, N_{i_1}^{(2)} \ldots \left\{ x_{(i_1 \ldots i_{d-1})i_d}^{(d)}, i_d = 1, N_{i_1 \ldots i_{d-1}}^{(d)} \right\} \right\} \right\}$$

However, each of the inner nested array elements, associated with an outer array index, is now independent in size and distribution of grid coordinates.

Figure 12-1 shows an example of a jagged 2-D grid structure defined as a 1-D array of 1-D arrays (or isolines).

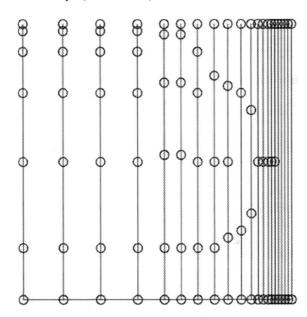

Figure 12-1. *Examples of 2-D ragged LUT*

The advantage of jagged grid arrays is the possibility to use an anisotropic distribution of grid points for optimal LUT data interpolation.

The structure of ragged arrays naturally leads to the implementation of a simple recursive 1-D interpolation and extrapolation process. The interpolation and extrapolation schemes always operate in a single dimension analogous to how the data was originally generated, so the interpolation and extrapolation schemes used may be specified on a per dimension basis. The lowest requirement is to have at least two points per isoline. In addition, the result of the bracketing, required to produce intermediate interpolation points, must also produce at least two points per subsequent lower dimension. One should be aware that too few sample points can cause interpolation errors. The number of sample points must be sufficient to reduce the error to an acceptable level.

Preparing Table Data

Ragged arrays are not native in Verilog-A. The lookup table data based on ragged array grids may be stored in a file or as a sequence of one-dimensional arrays or a single two-dimensional array. Here, we describe the formatting of table data in a file. The table data file may contain multiple dependent variables, all sharing the same jagged array grid.

A lookup table for m dependent variables of dimension d is laid out in $d+m$ data columns. The first d columns are used to specify coordinates of the d-dimensional jagged grid. It is followed by the m columns containing the values of dependent variables. The jagged grid coordinates are ordered from the outermost (slowest changing) coordinate to the innermost (fastest changing) coordinate. Though an isoline ordinate does not change for a given isoline, in this scheme the ordinate is repeated for each point of that isoline (thus keeping the input data as a set of data rows all with the same number of points). The result is a sequential listing of each isoline with the total number of rows in the listing being equal to the total number of jagged array grid points.

As an example, let us consider a lookup table data file for a function $f(x,y)=0.5x+y$:

```
# y x f(x,y)
#y=0 isoline
    0.0 1.0 0.5
    0.0 2.0 1.0
    0.0 3.0 1.5
    0.0 4.0 2.0
```

```
    0.0 5.0 2.5
    0.0 6.0 3.0
#y=0.5 isoline
    0.5 1.0 1.0
    0.5 3.0 2.0
    0.5 5.0 3.0
#y=1.0 isoline
    1.0 1.0 1.5
    1.0 2.0 2.0
    1.0 4.0 3.0
```

The table has only one dependent variable $f(x,y)$ on a 2-D jagged grid. There are three isolines for y values, 0.0, 0.5, and 1.0, while x is sampled at various points on each of the three isolines. The slowly changing outer independent variable appears to the left, while the rapidly changing inner independent variable appears to the right. Isoline ordinates are repeated for each sample on a given isoline. Each sample point is separated by a newline and each column is separated by one or more spaces or tabs. Comments in table data files begin with the # character and continue to the end of that line. They may appear anywhere in the file. Blank lines are ignored. The numbers in the table shall be real or integer literals.

It is suggested that the user arranges the sampled isolines in sorted order (one isoline following another in all dimensions). However, if the user provides the data in random order, the system will sort the data into isolines in each dimension. Whether the data is sorted or not, the system determines the isoline ordinate by reading its exact value from the file or array. Any noise on the isoline ordinate may cause the system to incorrectly generate multiple isolines where the user intended a single isoline. Within the data table, each row shall be distinct in terms of its jagged grid coordinate values. If there are two or more rows with the same grid coordinates and dependent variable values, then the duplicates shall be ignored and the simulator may generate a warning. If there are two or more rows with the same grid coordinate values but different dependent values, then an error is generated.

When the data source is represented as a sequence of 1-D arrays or a single 2-D array, the isolines are laid out conceptually the same way with each 1-D array, or a column of the 2-D array, being just a column in the file format described earlier. Arrays may be specified directly via the assignment patterns or array variable names.

Lookup Table Function

Once a data table is formatted in a file or assigned to Verilog-A arrays, it can be used to provide a LUT mapping:

$$\left(x^{(1)}, x^{(2)}, \ldots, x^{(d)} \right) \rightarrow y$$

where $(x^{(1)}, x^{(2)}, \ldots, x^{(d)})$ are independent input variables, while y is a required dependent output value. The mapping is performed by searching the data table for grid points closest to the given input and using these points to interpolate (or extrapolate) for the corresponding output value.

To perform LUT mapping, Verilog-A provides a multidimensional interpolation and lookup system function $table_model invoked by using one of the syntax forms:

```
$table_model ( input-variables, data-source )
$table_model ( input-variables, data-source, control-string )
```

The first syntax form requires to specify a set of input variables and a table data source. The state of the data source is captured on the first call to the $table_model function. Any change after this point is ignored.

The optional control string specifies how the interpolation and extrapolation are performed in the data table. If the control string is not specified, $table_model will perform linear interpolation and linear extrapolation in all dimensions.

Input Variables and Data Source

The *input-variables* are provided as a comma-separated list of expressions:

expression, ...

that evaluate a set of *d* input variables at which the lookup function should be evaluated. Any expression that can be assigned to an analog signal can be used here.

If the table data are stored in a file, the *data-source* is specified as a string literal:

" *file-name* "

specifying the name of the file.

The next example illustrates a simple call to the $table_model function using the table data file described in the previous section and stored as sample.tbl:

```
module lut_example(a, b);
    electrical a, b;
    inout a, b;
    analog begin
        I(a, b) <+ $table_model(0.0, V(a,b),
                                "sample.tbl");
    end
endmodule
```

The $table_model function is called specifying zero (0) for the *y* input variable and uses a module port potential difference as the *x* input variable.

Alternatively, the lookup table data source can be given as a comma-separated list of *d* one-dimensional array identifiers:

array-identifier, ...

each of them providing a corresponding column of table data in a text file. The module lut_example can be defined using one-dimensional arrays as

```
module lut_example(a, b);
    electrical a, b;
    inout a, b;
    real y[0:11], x[0:11], f_xy[0:11];
    analog initial
        begin
            // y=0.0 isoline
            y[0] =0.0; x[0] =1.0; f_xy[0] =0.5;
            y[1] =0.0; x[1] =2.0; f_xy[1] =1.0;
            y[2] =0.0; x[2] =3.0; f_xy[2] =1.5;
            y[3] =0.0; x[3] =4.0; f_xy[3] =2.0;
            y[4] =0.0; x[4] =5.0; f_xy[4] =2.5;
            y[5] =0.0; x[5] =6.0; f_xy[5] =3.0;

            // y=0.5 isoline
            y[6] =0.5; x[6] =1.0; f_xy[6] =1.0;
            y[7] =0.5; x[7] =3.0; f_xy[7] =2.0;
            y[8] =0.5; x[8] =5.0; f_xy[8] =3.0;

            // y=1.0 isoline
            y[9] =1.0; x[9] =1.0; f_xy[9] =1.5;
            y[10]=1.0; x[10]=2.0; f_xy[10]=2.0;
            y[11]=1.0; x[11]=4.0; f_xy[11]=3.0;
        end

    analog
```

```
      I(a, b)<+$table_model(0, V(a,b), y, x, f_xy);
endmodule
```

It is also possible to use assignment patterns here either for the array initialization or directly as $table_model function arguments. Finally, a single two-dimensional array identifier can be used as *data-source*:

```
real table[0:2][0:11] =
'{
  '{0.0,0.0,0.0,0.0,0.0,0.0,0.5,0.5,0.5,1.0,1.0,1.0},
  '{1.0,2.0,3.0,4.0,5.0,6.0,1.0,3.0,5.0,1.0,2.0,4.0},
  '{0.5,1.0,1.5,2.0,2.5,3.0,1.0,2.0,3.0,1.5,2.0,3.0}
};
...
I(a, b) <+ $table_model(0, V(a,b), table);
```

Here, a two-dimensional array with table data is initialized using nested assignment patterns.

Control String

The *control-string* specifies how interpolations are performed in each dimension and how they should extrapolate at the boundaries of each dimension. It also provides some control on how to treat columns of the input data source. It is defined by one of the string literals:

```
" control-character-set, ...   "
" control-character-set, ... ; dependent-selector "
```

The control strings contain a comma-separated list of control character sets followed by an optional semicolon and the expression *dependent-selector* that should evaluate as a constant integer. The control character sets provide control over each independent variable with the first set applying to the outermost coordinate and so on. The optional dependent variable selector is an integer number allowing us to specify which dependent variable in the data source we wish to interpolate. This number runs from *1* to *m* with *m* being the total number of dependent variables specified in the data source.

Each control character set associated with interpolation control string has at most three characters. The first character controls interpolation and as shown in the Table 12-1.

Table 12-1. *Interpolation control character*

Control Character	Description
I	Ignore this input column
D	Closest point (discrete) lookup
1	Linear interpolation (default)
2	Quadratic spline interpolation
3	Cubic spline interpolation

It is possible to ignore interpolation for the given input dimensions if it is annotated with the I control character. The closest point interpolation returns the closest point in the specified dimension. The linear interpolation algorithm provides a simple linear interpolation between the closest sample points on a given isoline. Cubic spline interpolation generates a spline for each isoline being interpolated. Quadratic splines are similar to cubic splines, offering more efficient evaluation with generally less favorable interpolation results. As a general rule, cubic splines are best applied to smoothly varying data (such as the DC I-V characteristic of a diode), while linear interpolation is a better option for data with abrupt transitions (such as a transient pulsed waveform).

The remaining characters in the control sub-string specify the extrapolation behavior of a LUT model when the value of input variables is outside the data table range. The extrapolation control characters are described in Table 12-2.

Table 12-2. *Extrapolation control character*

Control Character	Description
C	Constant extrapolation
L	Linear extrapolation (default)
E	Error on an extrapolation request

The constant extrapolation method returns the table endpoint value. Linear extrapolation extends linearly to the requested point from the endpoint using a slope consistent with the selected interpolation method. The user may also disable extrapolation by choosing the error extrapolation method. With this method, an extrapolation error is reported if the $table_model function is requested to evaluate a point beyond the interpolation region.

For each dimension, users may use up to two extrapolation method characters to specify the extrapolation method used for each end. When no extrapolation method character is given, the linear extrapolation method will be used for both ends as default. Error extrapolation results in a fatal error. When one extrapolation method character is given, the specified extrapolation method will be used for both ends. When two extrapolation method characters are given, the first character specifies the extrapolation method used for the end with the lower coordinate value, and the second character is used for the end with the higher coordinate value.

The specification of the extrapolation control characters could be also essential for the correct generation of spline interpolation coefficients. If the constant extrapolation is specified, the endpoint derivative is set to zero, thus avoiding a discontinuity in the first-order derivative at that endpoint. If the user selects linear extrapolation, this leads to natural splines.

Some examples of control strings are shown in Table 12-3.

185

Table 12-3. *Example control strings*

Control String	Description
"" or control string omitted	Null string, default linear interpolation, and extrapolation. The dimensionality of the data is assumed to be N. Column $N+1$ is taken as the dependent
"1L,1L"	Data is 2-D, linear interpolation and extrapolation in both dimensions
"1LL,1LL"	Same as before, an extrapolation method specified for both ends in each dimension
"1LL,1LL;1"	Same as before, dependent variable 1 is specified. This is the default behavior when there are multiple dependent variables in the file and there is no dependent variable selector specified in the control string
"D,1,3"	Closest point lookup in the outer dimension, linear interpolation on dimension two, and cubic spline interpolation on the inner dimension
"I,1CC,1CC;3"	Ignore column 1, linear interpolation, and constant extrapolation in all dimensions; interpolation applies to dependent variable 3. There are at least six columns in the data file
"3,D,I,1;3"	Cubic spline interpolation in dimension 3 (column 1), closest lookup in dimension 2 (column 2), ignore column 3, and use linear interpolation on the innermost dimension (dimension 1, column 4). Interpolate dependent variable 3 (column 7). This file has at least seven columns
"C,,3"	Data is 3-D, equivalent to "1CC, 1LL, 3LL"

The following example implements a simple LUT MOSFET transistor model:

```
module nfet(d, g, s);
    inout d, g, s;
    electrical d, g, s;

    parameter string int_exp = "3LL,3LL";
    real Ids, Cgs, Cgd;

    analog begin
        Ids = $table_model(V(d,s), (V(g,s)),
                            "Id.tbl", int_exp);
        Cgd = $table_model(V(d,s), (V(g,s)),
                            "Cg.tbl", "1LL,1LL:2");
        Cgs = $table_model(V(d,s), (V(g,s)),
                            "Cg.tbl", "1LL,1LL:1");
        I(d,s) <+ Ids;
        I(g,d) <+ Cgd * ddt(V(g,d));
        I(g,s) <+ Cgs * ddt(V(g,s));
    end
endmodule
```

Here, the two separate table data files are used for the current and capacitance modeling. The string parameter int_exp allows external control of the LUT control string.

CHAPTER 13

Small-Signal Functions

Thus far we have been focused on large signal modeling with Verilog-A in the time domain. A large signal is any signal having enough magnitude to reveal a branch's nonlinear behavior. A small signal analysis assumes that variations in signal potential and flow amplitudes are so small that the branch constitutive relationship can be assumed to behave linearly. Practically, the small signal analysis models are obtained by linearization of the nonlinear branch constitutive relationships near a static operation point. It allows performing the small signal analysis in the frequency domain solving algebraic rather than differential equations.

Because the focus of this book is the Verilog-A language and its use, we will not go into theoretical details behind the frequency domain small-signal analysis. Readers seeking additional information should check the standard textbooks in this area. In this chapter, we will just introduce Verilog-A functions that can be used to provide small-signal stimuli in the frequency domain for the AC and noise small-signal analysis.

© Slobodan Mijalković 2022
S. Mijalković, *A Practical Guide to Verilog-A*, https://doi.org/10.1007/978-1-4842-6351-8_13

AC Analysis

The abbreviation AC (from Alternating Current in electrical engineering) is commonly used to specify a sinusoidal signal waveform:

$$v(t) = M \cos(\omega t + \phi)$$

where M is the amplitude, ϕ is the phase, and ω is the frequency of the AC signal. The AC analysis assumes that a linearized small-signal model is subjected to a one or more sinusoidal signal stimuli. In that case, all the branch potentials and flow signals are also sinusoidal with the same frequency as the stimulus but with their own magnitude and phase.

In the frequency domain a sinusoidal signals is represented as a phasor

$$V = Me^{j\phi}$$

being a vector in a complex plane defined by the sinusoidal signal magnitude and phase. Given the frequency provided by the simulator, AC analysis solves a set of algebraic equation for the signals' magnitude and phases instead of solving differential equations for the signal waveforms in time domain. It is important to understand that in AC analysis not only the branch signals but also real type variables, depending on the signal values, are implicitly converted to complex phasor variables defined by two numbers (magnitude and phase). In order for us to be able to introduces the sinusoidal signals into AC analysis, Verilog-A provides the AC stimulus function.

AC Stimulus Function

The sinusoidal stimulus in the frequency domain is provided using the ac_stim() function. It can be used in one of the syntax forms:

```
ac_stim ()
ac_stim ( analysis-name )
```

```
ac_stim ( analysis-name , mag )
ac_stim ( analysis-name , mag , phase )
```

The argument *analysis-name* is a string constant specifying the name of a small-signal analysis. The small-signal analysis name depends on the simulator but the expected (and default) value for the *analysis-name* is "ac". When the name of the simulator small-signal analysis matches *analysis-name*, the AC stimulus function becomes active and returns the phasor with the magnitude and phase defined by the function arguments *mag* and *phase*, respectively. The magnitude argument *mag* has no physical unit and has a default value of 1. The *phase* argument is given in radians and its default value is 0. It makes the following calls to the AC stimulus identical:

```
ac_stim();
ac_stim("ac");
ac_stim("ac", 1.0);
ac_stim("ac", 1.0, 0.0);
```

The AC stimulus function returns 0 during large-signal static and transient analyses in the time domain. This allows us to use AC stimulus functions in expressions with no effect except in small signal analysis. For example, in the branch contribution statement:

```
V(p, n) <+ R * I(p, n) + ac_stim("ac", m1);
```

the ac_stim() function adds the AC small signal stimulus with magnitude m1 and phase 0 in parallel to the linear resistor branch. It will become active only during "ac" analysis and does not affect the branch contribution statement in other analyses.

We should keep in mind that the AC stimulus function returns a phasor as a unitless complex numerical value that can be also assigned to the module variable. The previous contribution statement can be also defined as

```
v_ac = ac_stim("ac", m1);
V(p, n) <+ R * I(p, n) + v_ac;
```

where v_ac is previously declared real variable.

Noise Analysis

When we model the behavior of an analog system, we often need to analyze the system's sensitivity to various noise stimuli. The term noise, as it is used here, denotes small-signal statistical fluctuations of branch potential and flow values. To model and analyze the effects of the large-signal noise fluctuations, one could consider using the $arandom system tasks as described in Chapter 11.

The concept of phasors used in AC analysis can be also employed for the small-signal noise analysis. However, the phase of the phasors that effectively represent small signal noise signals are subject to random variation from 0 to 2π radians, and the phasor magnitude is frequency dependent. For that reason, noise stimuli stimuli are specified in noise analysis using the power spectral density (PSD), which is the mean square of the noise signal magnitude within a frequency interval of 1 Hz.

Verilog-A provides several noise stimuli functions to support different noise PSD frequency dependences in noise analysis. These noise functions are often referred to as noise sources. Similar to AC stimulus function, the noise sources are only active in small-signal noise analysis and return 0 otherwise.

White Noise Function

White noise stochastic processes are those whose current value is completely uncorrelated with any previous or future values. This implies their PSD of the white noise does not depend on frequency. The white noise sources are introduced in the noise analysis using the white_noise() function in one of the syntax forms:

white_noise (*pwr*)
white_noise (*pwr* , *name*)

The argument *pwr* specifies the frequency-independent PSD of the white noise source. The optional argument *name* is a string constant that acts as a label for the noise source. It could be used by the simulator to output the individual contribution of each noise source to the total output noise. To this end, the contributions of noise sources with the same name from the same instance of a module are combined in the noise contribution summary.

In the following example, the module bridge implements the bridge network with two noisy resistors.

```
module bridge(p, n);
    inout p, n;
    electrical p, n, mc, ml;
    parameter real R = 1.0 from (0:inf);
    parameter real C = 1.0p from [0:inf);
    parameter real L = 1.0p from [0:inf);

    real wnval, wnpower;

    analog begin
        wnpower = (4.0 * `P_K * $temperature) / R;

        I(p,mc) <+ V(p,mc) / R + white_noise(wnpower);
```

```
        wnval = white_noise(wnpower, "thermal");
        I(p, ml) <+ V(p, ml) / R + wnval;

        I(mc, n) <+ C * ddt(V(mc, n));
        V(ml, n) <+ L * ddt(I(ml, n));
    end
endmodule
```

Note that the noise sources are basically functions that could be used anywhere in the analog procedural expressions. For the first resistor, the noise sources is introduced directly in the branch contribution expression while for the second resistor the return value of the noise source function is first assigned to a variable wnval, which is then used in the resistor branch contribution statement. Although both white noise sources are using the same PSD value, they are completely uncorrelated.

Flicker Noise Function

The flicker_noise() function models the noise sources using one of the syntax form:

```
flicker_noise ( pwr , exp )
flicker_noise ( pwr , exp , name )
```

It can be used to generates the noise with a power spectral density of *pwr* which varies in proportion to $1/f^{exp}$ where *exp* is the second argument of the flicker noise function and $f = \omega/2\pi$ is the frequency. The optional argument *name* is a string constant that acts as noise source label.

The use of the Flicker noise source function is demonstrated in the noisy_diode module:

```
module noisy_diode(a,b);
    inout a, b;
    electrical a, b;
```

```
parameter real af = 1;
parameter real kf = 1;
parameter real is = 1e-14;

real af;

analog begin
    pwr_1 = kf * pow(abs(Id), af);
    I(a,b) <+ is * (exp(V(a,b) / $vt) - 1) +
        white_noise(2 * `P_Q * abs(Id), "shot") +
        flicker_noise(pwr_1, 1.0, "flicker");
end
endmodule
```

Here the white_noise() function is used to contribute the diode shot noise and the flicker_noise() function to add the flicker noise with $1/f$ dependence of the PSD.

On should be careful with the specification of the PSD in the Flicker noise source functions when the bias applied to the branch changes sign[1].

Look-Up Table Noise Functions

Verilog-A provides two look-up table noise functions: noise_table() and noise_table_log() to interpolate the frequency dependent noise PSD from the pre-defined table data.

---

[1] G. J. Coram, C. C. McAndrew, K. K. Gullapalli and K. S. Kundert, "Flicker Noise Formulations in Compact Models," in IEEE Transactions on Computer-Aided Design of Integrated Circuits and Systems, vol. 39, no. 10, pp. 2812-2821, Oct. 2020, doi: 10.1109/TCAD.2020.2966444.

The `noise_table()` function interpolates a set of values to model a process where the spectral density of the noise varies as a piecewise linear function of frequency using the syntax:

```
noise-table ( data )
noise-table ( data , name )
```

On the other hand, the `noise_table_log()` function interpolates a set of values to model a process where the spectral density of the noise varies as a piecewise linear function of the base-10 logarithm of the frequency using the syntax:

```
noise-table-log ( data )
noise-table-log ( data , name )
```

The *data* input argument can either be a real vector or a string indicating a filename. When the input is a real vector it contains a sequence of pairs of real numbers: the first number in each pair is the frequency in Hz and the second is the power in W. The vector can either be specified as an array parameter or an array assignment pattern. The optional argument *name* is a string constant that acts as a noise source label.

When the *data* argument is a file name, the indicated file will contain the frequency/power pairs. The filename argument shall be constant and will be either a string literal or a string parameter. Each frequency/power pair shall be separated by a newline and the numbers in the pair shall be separated by one or more spaces or tabs. To increase the readability of the data file, comments may be inserted before or after any frequency/power pair. Comments begin with # character and end with a newline. The input file shall be in text format only and the numbers shall be real or integer.

The following shows an example of the input file:

```
# noise_table_input.tbl
# Example of input file format for noise_table
#
# freq pwr
```

```
1.0e0 1.657580e-23
1.0e1 3.315160e-23
1.0e2 6.636320e-23
1.0e3 1.326064e-22
1.0e4 2.652128e-22
1.0e5 5.304256e-22
1.0e6 1.060851e-21
# End of the example input file.
```

Although the user is encouraged to specify each noise pair in order of ascending frequency, the simulator shall internally sort the pairs into ascending frequency if required. Each frequency value must be unique. The optional *name* argument acts as a label for the noise source as in the other noise source functions.

The noise_table() performs piecewise linear interpolation to compute the power spectral density generated by the function at each frequency between the lowest and highest frequency in the set of values. For frequencies lower than the lowest frequency in the value set, noise_table() returns the power specified for the lowest frequency, and for frequencies higher than the highest frequency, noise_table() returns the power specified for the highest frequency.

The noise_table_log() interpolates the values of the power spectral density logarithmically. For a given frequency f the noise power shall be computed using the two pairs $(f1, p1)$ and $(f2, p2)$ in the input (whether an array or file), where $f1$ is the largest frequency value in the input data less than f and $f2$ is the smallest frequency larger than f (that is, $f1 < f < f2$). The noise power P is interpolated as:

$$P = \left(10, \log(p1) + \left(\log(p2) - \log(p1)\right) \cdot \frac{\log f / f_1}{\log f_2 / f_1}\right.$$

As with `noise_table()`, for frequencies lower than the lowest frequency in the value set, `noise_table_log()` returns the power specified for the lowest frequency, and for frequencies higher than the highest frequency, `noise_table_log()` returns the power specified for the highest frequency.

The difference between `noise_table` and `noise_table_log` is illustrated in Figure 13-1.

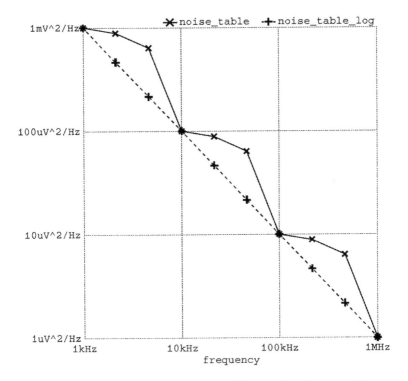

Figure 13-1. *Comparison of `noise_table` and `noise_table_log`*

The `noise_table_log` function produces a straight line on a log-log plot from just two points:

```
noise_table_log('{1,1, 1e6,1e-6});
```

whereas the linear interpolation of noise_table() function call:

```
noise_table('{1,1, 1e1, 1e-1, 1e2,
              1e-2, 1e3, 1e-3, 1e4,
              1e-4, 1e5, 1e-5, 1e6, 1e-6});
```

produces a series of curves between the interpolating points.

Correlated Noise Sources

Each noise source function generates noise that is uncorrelated with the noise generated by other noise source functions. In order to get perfectly correlated noise in two branch contribution statements we can assign the output of one noise function to a variable and then use the variable in the branch contribution statements as demonstrated in the following example:

```
n = white_noise(pwr);
V(a,b) <+ c1 * n;
V(c,d) <+ c2 * n;
```

The white noise contribution in (a,b) and (c,d) branches is perfectly correlated.

Partially correlated noise is generated by combining the output of shared and unshared noise functions, as demonstrated in the example:

```
n1 = white_noise(1-corr);
n2 = white_noise(1-corr);
n12 = white_noise(corr);
V(a,b) <+ Kv*(n1 + n12);
I(b,c) <+ Ki*(n2 + n12);
```

The level of correlation is defined by the variable corr. For corr=1 the white noise sources in the branches (a,b) and (c,d) are perfectly correlated while for corr=1 they are uncorrelated.

CHAPTER 14

Filters

Verilog-A filters are analog operators that remove some unwanted components or features from a signal. Similar to functions, filters take arguments at the input and return a value. However, as with other Verilog-A analog operators, filters also maintain their internal states and their output is a function of both the input arguments and the internal states. Verilog-A supports filters in the time and frequency domain.

Time-Domain Filters

Verilog-A provides a set of time-domain filters that can be used to delay signals and to remove discontinuity or bound rate of change of the signal waveforms.

Absolute Delay Filter

The absolute delay filter implements the transport delay for signal waveforms. The syntax of the absolute delay filter is

```
absdelay ( expression , delay )
absdelay ( expression , delay, maxdelay )
```

The filter output is the input *expression* delayed by the time *delay* as shown in Figure 14-1.

© Slobodan Mijalković 2022
S. Mijalković, *A Practical Guide to Verilog-A*, https://doi.org/10.1007/978-1-4842-6351-8_14

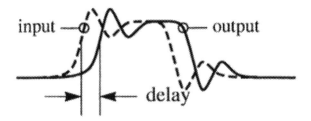

Figure 14-1. *Absolute delay filter input-output transformation*

The *delay* shall be specified a positive number. If the optional argument *maxdelay* is not specified, the value of *delay*, when the absdelay() is evaluated for the first time, will be used and any future changes to *delay* will be ignored. If the argument *maxdelay* is specified, then *delay* can be modified in the subsequent absdelay() calls. If *delay* is greater than *maxdelay*, *maxdelay* will be used as a substitute for *delay*.

In DC and operating point analyses, absdelay() returns the value of the *expression*. In frequency-domain AC and noise analyses, the absolute delay filter shifts the phase of the input *expression* by the value of $\omega \cdot delay$ where ω is the angular frequency.

Transition Filter

The transition filter is used to smooth out piecewise constant waveforms by introducing transitions and delays that stretch instantaneous changes in signals over a finite amount of time and can delay the transitions. The syntax of the transition filter is

```
transition( expression )
transition( expression , delay )
transition( expression , delay, rise-time )
transition( expression , delay, rise-time, fall-time )
transition( expression , delay, rise-time, fall-time,
time-tol )
```

The input arguments, *delay*, *rise-time*, *fall-time*, and *time-tol*, are optional, but if specified shall be non-negative.

The transition filter converts a piecewise constant waveform given by the input argument *expression* into a piecewise linear output waveform as shown in Figure 14-2.

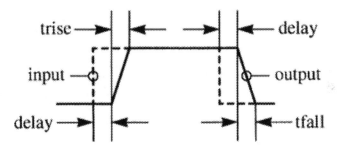

Figure 14-2. *Transition filter input-output transformation*

The transition filter forces all positive transitions of the *expression* to occur over *rise-time* and all negative transitions to occur in *fall-time* after an initial time *delay*. If *delay* is not specified, it is assumed to be 0. If only a positive *rise-time* value is specified, the simulator uses it for both rise and fall times. If neither *rise-time* nor *fall-time* is specified or set to be 0, the rise and fall times default to the value defined by the currently active `default_transition` compiler directive, which is introduced in Chapter 20. Otherwise, the ideal behavior of a zero-duration transition using very small but nonzero transition times shall apply. The time tolerance *time-tol* argument specifies the maximum allowable error between the true transition point and one selected by the simulator. If *time-tol* is not specified, the transition function causes the simulator to assure that each transition is adequately resolved.

Note   Even though the first derivative of the transition filter output waveform is discontinuous, it is not necessary to announce discontinuities using the $discontinuity system task (see Chapter 16) because the transition filter takes responsibility for notifying the simulator of the discontinuities that it produces.

In DC analysis, transition() passes the value of the *expression* directly to its output. Because the transition function cannot be linearized in general, it is not possible to accurately represent a transition filter output signal in AC analysis. The AC transfer function of the transition filter is approximately modeled as having unity transmission for all frequencies in all situations.

Since transitions take some time to complete, a new transition can be specified before a previously specified transition is complete. In this case, the transition function terminates the previous transition and shifts to the new one in such a way that the continuity of the output waveform is maintained. With different delays, a new transition can be activated before a previously specified transition starts. The transition function handles this by deleting any transitions which would follow a newly scheduled transition. A transition function can have an arbitrary number of transitions pending.

Slew Filter

The slew analog filters bound the rate of change, or slope, of the signal waveform. A typical use of the slew filter is to generate continuous signals from piecewise continuous signals. The syntax of the slew filter is

```
slew ( expression )
slew ( expression , max-pos-slope )
slew ( expression , max-pos-slope, max-neg-slope )
```

The value of *max-pos-slope* shall be positive and *max-neg-slope* shall be negative.

When applied, the slew filter forces all transitions of input *expression* faster than *max-pos-slope* not to exceed *max-pos-slope* for positive transitions and limits the negative transitions to the maximum negative slew rate *max_neg_slope* as shown in Figure 14-3.

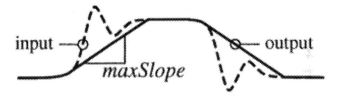

Figure 14-3. *Slew filter input-output transformation*

If the *max-neg-slew-rate* is not specified, it defaults to the opposite of the *max-pos-slew-rate*. If no rates are specified, the slew() filter passes the signal through unchanged. If the rate of change of *expression* is less than the specified maximum slew rates, slew() returns the value of the input expression.

In DC analysis, slew() simply passes the value of the *expression* to its output. During a small-signal analysis, such as AC or noise analysis, the slew filter has a unity transfer function from the first argument to the output when not slewing and 0 transfer function when slewing.

Frequency-Domain Filters

It is often convenient to specify the filters in the frequency domain using the Laplace transform or the Z-transform. The Laplace transform and Z-transform filters are expressed as rational functions of complex variables defined in s-plane and z-plane complex domains.

The frequency-domain filters in the Verilog-A language are available in the zero-pole, zero-denominator, numerator-pole, and numerator-denominator formulations.

Some of the arguments in calls to frequency-domain filters are expected to be arrays. An array can either be passed as an array identifier (e.g., an array parameter or an array variable) or an array assignment pattern. The zeros argument may be represented as a null argument. The null argument is characterized by two adjacent commas (, ,) in the argument list.

Laplace Transform Filters

The Laplace transform filters implement linear continuous-time network functions. Each filter takes an optional parameter ε, which is a real number or a nature used for deriving an absolute tolerance. Whether an absolute tolerance is needed depends on the context where the filter is used.

Zero-Pole Filter

The Laplace zero-pole filter form is introduced with the syntax:

```
laplace_zp ( expr , ζ, ρ )
laplace_zp ( expr , ζ, ρ, ε )
```

where ζ is a vector of M pairs of real numbers. Each pair represents a zero as a complex number. The first number in the pair is the real part of the zero and the second is the imaginary part. Similarly, ρ is the vector of N real pairs, one for each complex pole. The poles are given in the same manner as the zeros.

The zero-pole transfer function is defined as

$$H(s) = \frac{\displaystyle\prod_{k=0}^{M-1}\left(1 - \frac{s}{\zeta_k^\gamma + j\zeta_k^i}\right)}{\displaystyle\prod_{k=0}^{M-1}\left(1 - \frac{s}{\rho_k^\gamma + j\rho_k^i}\right)}$$

where ζ_k^γ and ζ_k^i are real and imaginary parts of the kth zero, while ρ_k^γ and ρ_k^i are the real and imaginary parts of the kth pole. If a root (a pole or zero) is real, the imaginary part shall be specified as zero. If a root is complex, its conjugate shall also be present. If a root is zero, then the term associated with it is implemented as s, rather than $(1 - s/\gamma)$, where r is the root.

For example:

```
V(out) <+ laplace_zp(V(in), '{-1,0}, '{-1,-1,-1,1});
```

implements

$$H(s) = \frac{1+s}{\left(1 + \dfrac{s}{1+j}\right)\left(1 + \dfrac{s}{1-j}\right)}$$

Note the use of assignment patterns to pass array arguments to the filter function.

Zero-Denominator Filter

The syntax for the zero-denominator Laplace filter is

```
laplace_zd ( expr, ζ, d )
laplace_zd ( expr, ζ, d, ε )
```

where ζ is a vector of M pairs of real numbers. Each pair represents a zero; the first number in the pair is the real part of the zero and the second is the imaginary part. Similarly, d is the vector of real numbers containing the coefficients of the denominator.

The zero-denominator transfer function is defined as

$$H(s) = \frac{\prod\limits_{k=0}^{M-1}\left(1 - \dfrac{s}{\zeta_k^\gamma + j\zeta_k^i}\right)}{\sum\limits_{k=0}^{N-1} d_s s^k}$$

where ζ_k^γ and ζ_k^i are real and imaginary parts of the kth zero, while d_k is the coefficient of the kth power of s in the denominator. If a zero is real, the imaginary part shall be specified as zero. If a zero is complex, its conjugate shall also be present. If a zero has a zero value, then the term associated with it is implemented as s, rather than $(1 - s/\zeta)$.

Numerator-Pole Filter

The numerator-pole Laplace filter has a syntax:

```
laplace_np ( expr, n, ρ)
laplace_np ( expr, n, ρ, ε )
```

where n is a vector of M real numbers containing the coefficients of the numerator. Similarly, ρ is a vector of N pairs of real numbers. Each pair represents a pole; the first number in the pair is the real part of the pole and the second is the imaginary part.

The numerator-pole transfer function is defined as

$$H(s) = \frac{\sum\limits_{k=0}^{M-1} n_k s^k}{\prod\limits_{k=0}^{M-1}\left(1 - \dfrac{s}{\rho_k^\gamma + j\rho_k^i}\right)}$$

where n_k is the coefficient of the kth power of s in the numerator, while ρ_k^γ and ρ_k^i are the real and imaginary parts of the kth pole. If a pole is real, the imaginary part shall be specified with a zero value. If a pole is complex, its conjugate shall also be present. If a pole has a zero value, then the term associated with it is implemented as s, rather than $(1 = s/\rho)$.

For example, a numerator-pole Laplace filter in the contribution statement

```
V(out) <+ laplace_np( V(in), '{ 1 },
         '{
             -0.81,  0.59,
             -0.81, -0.59,
             -0.31,  0.95,
             -0.31, -0.95,
             -1.0,   0.0
         }
);
```

realizes the fifth-order Butterworth filter.

Numerator-Denominator Filter

The numerator-denominator Laplace filter has the syntax:

```
laplace_nd ( expr, n, d )
laplace_nd ( expr, n, d, ε )
```

where n is a vector of M real numbers containing the coefficients of the numerator and d is a vector of N real numbers containing the coefficients of the denominator.

The numerator-denominator transfer function is defined as

$$H(s) = \frac{\displaystyle\sum_{k=0}^{M-1} n_k s^k}{\displaystyle\sum_{k=0}^{M-1} d_k s^k}$$

where n_k is the coefficient of the kth power of s in the numerator and d_k is the coefficient of the kth of s in the denominator.

For example, the contribution statement with the integral operator in the time domain

```
V(out) < + idt(Ku * V(in) - Kp * V(out));
```

can be alternatively implemented as

```
V(out) <+ laplace_nd(V(in), '{ Ku }, '{ Kp, 1 });
```

using the Laplace numerator-denominator filter.

The Z-Transform Filters

The Z-transform filters implement linear discrete-time filters. Each filter supports a parameter T that specifies the sampling period of the filter. A filter with a unity transfer function acts like a simple sample-and-hold that samples every T second and exhibits no delay.

All Z-transform filters share three common arguments: T, τ, and t_0. T specifies the period of the filter, is mandatory, and shall be positive. τ specifies the transition time, is optional, and shall be non-negative. If the transition time is specified and is nonzero, the time step is controlled to accurately resolve both the leading and the trailing corner of the transition. If it is not specified, the transition time is defined by the `default_transition` compiler directive (introduced in Chapter 20), and the time step is not controlled to resolve the trailing corner of the transition. If the transition time is specified as zero (0), then the output is abruptly discontinuous. A Z-transform filter with zero transition time shall not be directly assigned to a branch. Finally, t_0 specifies the time of the first transition and is also optional. If not given, the first transition occurs at $t = 0$.

Zero-Pole Filter

The zero-pole form of the Z-transform filter is called with the syntax:

```
zi_zp ( expr , ζ, ρ, T )
zi_zp ( expr , ζ, ρ, T, τ)
zi_zp ( expr , ζ, ρ, T, τ, t₀)
```

where ζ is a vector of M pairs of real numbers. Each pair represents a zero; the first number in the pair is the real part of the zero and the second is the imaginary part. Similarly, ρ is the vector of N real pairs, one for each pole. The poles are given in the same manner as the zeros.

The zero-pole transfer function is defined as

$$H(z) = \frac{\prod_{k=0}^{M-1} 1 - z^{-1}\left(\zeta_k^\gamma + j\zeta_k^i\right)}{\prod_{k=0}^{N-1} 1 - z^{-1}\left(\rho_k^\gamma + j\rho_k^i\right)}$$

where ζ_k^γ and ζ_k^i are the real and imaginary parts of the kth zero, while ρ_k^γ and ρ_k^i are real and imaginary parts of the kth pole. If a root (a pole or zero) is real, the imaginary part shall be specified as zero. If a root is complex, its conjugate shall also be present. If a root is zero (0), then the term associated with it is implemented as z, rather than (1 − z/γ), where r is the root.

For example, the contribution statement

```
V(out) <+ zi_zp(V(in), {0, 0}, {-1, 0});
```

implements the transfer function $H(z) = \dfrac{z^{-1}}{1+z^{-1}}$.

Zero-Denominator Filter

The zero-denominator form of the Z-transform filter is called with the syntax:

```
zi_zd ( expr, ζ, d, T)
zi_zd ( expr, ζ, d, T, τ)
zi_zd ( expr, ζ, d, T, τ, t₀)
```

where ζ is a vector of M pairs of real numbers. Each pair represents a zero; the first number in the pair is the real part of the zero and the second is the imaginary part. Similarly, d is the vector of N real numbers containing the coefficients of the denominator.

The zero-denominator transfer function is defined as

$$H(z) = \frac{\prod\limits_{k=0}^{M-1} 1 - z^{-1}\left(\zeta_k^\gamma + j\zeta_k^i\right)}{\sum\limits_{k=0}^{N-1} d_k z^{-k}}$$

where ζ_k^γ and ζ_k^i are the real and imaginary parts of the kth zero, while d_k is a coefficient of the kth power of s in the denominator. If a zero is real, the imaginary part shall be specified as zero. If a zero is complex, its conjugate shall also be present. If a zero is zero, then the term associated with it is implemented as z, rather than ($1 - z/\zeta$).

Numerator-Pole Filter

The numerator-pole form of the Z-transform filter is called with the syntax:

```
zi_np ( expr , n, ρ, T )
zi_np ( expr , n, ρ, T, τ)
zi_np ( expr , n, ρ, T, τ, t₀ )
```

where *n* is a vector of *M* real numbers containing the coefficients of
the numerator. Similarly, ρ is a vector of *N* pairs of real numbers. Each pair
represents a pole; the first number in the pair is the real part of the pole
and the second is the imaginary part.

The numerator-pole transfer function is defined as

$$H(z) = \frac{\displaystyle\sum_{k=0}^{M-1} n_k z^{-k}}{\displaystyle\prod_{k=0}^{N-1} 1 - z^{-1}\left(\rho_k^{\gamma} + j\rho_k^{i}\right)}$$

where n_k is the coefficient of the *k*th power of *s* in the numerator, while
ρ_k^{γ} and ρ_k^{i} are the real and imaginary parts of the *k*th pole. If a pole is
real, the imaginary part shall be specified as zero. If a pole is complex, its
conjugate shall also be present. If a pole is zero, then the term associated
with it is implemented as *z*, rather than ($1 - z/\rho$).

Numerator-Denominator Filter

The numerator-denominator form of the Z-transform filter is called with
the syntax:

```
zi_nd ( expr , n, d, T )
zi_nd ( expr , n, d, T, τ )
zi_nd ( expr , n, d, T, τ, t₀ )
```

where *n* is a vector of *M* real numbers containing the coefficients of the numerator and *d* is a vector of *N* real numbers containing the coefficients of the denominator.

The numerator-denominator transfer function is defined as

$$H(z) = \frac{\displaystyle\sum_{k=0}^{M-1} n_k z^{-k}}{\displaystyle\sum_{k=0}^{N-1} d_k z^{-k}}$$

where n_k is the coefficient of the *k*th power of *s* in the numerator and d_k is the coefficient of the *k*th power of *s* in the denominator.

For example, the contribution statement

```
V(out) <+ zi_nd(V(in), '{1}, '{0, -1});
```

implements the transfer function $H(z) = \dfrac{1}{1 - z^{-1}}$.

CHAPTER 15

Events

The behavior of a Verilog-A component can be controlled using events. An event is an occurrence of a particular change in the simulation stage or state of the component. The events have the characteristics of no time duration and events can be triggered and detected in different parts of the Verilog-A code evaluation.

Event Control Statements

Event control statements provide a means of watching for a change in a value. The events are introduced into Verilog-A procedural code by event control statements having syntax:

```
@ ( event-expression ) procedural-statement ;
```

An event control statement is specified with the punctuator @, or at sign. It is followed by the specification of an event expression in parentheses and a single procedural statement. The parentheses around the *event-expression* are required. Empty event specifications

```
@ ( ) procedural-statement ;
```

are not allowed as well as nested event control statements.

© Slobodan Mijalković 2022
S. Mijalković, *A Practical Guide to Verilog-A*, https://doi.org/10.1007/978-1-4842-6351-8_15

An event control statement looks for the desired change in the *event-expression*. When such a change (or event) occurs, an action is taken by executing the *procedural-statement*. The event detection is non-blocking, meaning the execution of the event procedural statement is skipped unless the event has occurred.

It is allowed to use event control statements in analog procedural blocks, along with other procedural statements, but with some restrictions. Event control statements cannot be used inside conditional statements unless the conditional expression is constant. Looping statements, analog initial blocks, and paramsets shall not contain event control statements.

Similar to analog procedural blocks and user-defined functions, event control statements are restricted to a single procedural statement. Multiple procedural statements are possible if encapsulated within a single procedural block statement. However, certain restrictions apply to a procedural statement that can be specified within an event control statement. The analog operators (derivative and integral operators, filters, etc.) cannot be used as part of the event control statement. An event control statement cannot maintain the internal states required by analog operators since it is only executed intermittently when the corresponding event is triggered. The branch contribution statements cannot be used inside an event control block because they could introduce discontinuities in signal waveforms.

The event expression consists of one or more event functions, separated by keywords "OR" or "or":

event-function or *event-function* OR ...

where both lowercase and uppercase keywords are allowed. The event functions can be also separated by commas:

event-function, event-function, ...

The "OR-ing" of event functions (or putting them in a comma-separated list) indicates that the occurrence of any one of the specified event functions shall trigger the execution of the event procedural statement. There are two types of event functions:

- Global event functions

- Monitored event functions

defining the corresponding global and monitored events.

Global Event Functions

Global events are generated by a simulator at various stages of the simulation. The user model cannot generate these events. These events are detected by using the names of the global event functions in an event expression. There are two global event functions predefined in Verilog-A: initial-step and final-step functions. The syntax of these functions is

```
initial_step
initial_step ( "analysis-identifier", ... )

final_step
final_step ( "analysis-identifier", ... )
```

Both global event functions can be used without arguments (and parentheses) or they can take a list of strings as optional arguments.

The strings in the argument list are compared to the name of the analysis being run. If any string matches the name of the current analysis name, the simulator generates an event. The initial_step function will trigger an event on the first point and the final_step function at the last point of that particular analysis. The final_step function will also generate a global event upon the termination of the simulation due to a $finish() simulation control task introduced in Chapter 16. In the examples:

```
initial_step( "ac", "noise", "dc" )
final_step( "tran" )
```

the initial_step function triggers events at the beginning of AC, Noise, and DC analyses, while the final_step function triggers an event at the end of a transient analysis. The supported analysis names in Verilog-A are given in Table 16-1. If no analysis list is specified, the initial_step global event is active during the solution of the first point of every analysis. The final_step global event, without an analysis list, will be active during the solution of the last point of every analysis.

The global event functions are useful when performing actions that should only occur at the beginning or the end of an analysis. As an example of using the initial_step function, let us consider the module skin_effect:[1]

```
module skin_effect (p, n);
    parameter integer lumps = 10 from (1:30];
    parameter real f0=1 from (0:inf);
    parameter real f 1=10 from (f0:inf);
    parameter real r0=1 from (0:inf);

    electrical p, n;
    inout t1, t2;

    real mult, mult2, wp, wz;
    real zeros[0:2*lumps-1], poles[0:2*lumps-1);
    integer i;
```

[1] K. Kundert and O. Zinke, The Designer's Guide to Verilog-AMS, The Designer's Guide Book Series, Springer, 2004.

```
analog begin
    @ (initial_step) begin
        mult = pow(f1/f0, 1.0/(4*lumps));
        mult2 = mult*mult;
        wz = 2*`M_PI*mult*f0;
        wp = mult2*wz;
        for(i=0; i < lumps; i=i+1) begin
            zeros[2*i] = -wz;
            zeros[2*i+1] = 0;
            poles[2*i] = -wp;
            poles[2*i+1] = 0;
            wz = mult2 * wp;
            wp = mult2 * wz;
        end
    end
    V(p,n) <+ r0*laplace_zp(1(p,n),zeros,poles);
end
endmodule
```

The initial_step function in the module skin_effect triggers the calculation of the poles and zeros used by the Laplace filter. Since the poles and zeros never change, they only need to be calculated once at the beginning of the analysis. As such, the initial_step function is used to increase the efficiency of the model. Without it, the poles and zeros would be recalculated at every time point, a substantial waste of time.

Monitored Event Functions

Monitored events are detected using event functions monitoring changes in signals, simulation time, or other runtime conditions. The monitored events differ from the standard control flow constructs (if-else or case) in the Verilog-A language in that the event generation and detection require satisfying accuracy constraints. The accuracy constraints can be either in value or time. Verilog-A offers three event monitoring functions: cross, above, and timer event functions.

Cross Function

The cross function is used for generating a monitored event to detect when an expression crosses 0 in the specified direction. In addition, the cross function controls the time step to accurately resolve the crossing.

The cross function can be used in one of the following syntax forms:

```
cross ( expression )
cross ( expression, direction )
cross ( expression, direction , time-tol )
cross ( expression, direction , time-tol , expr-tol )
cross ( expression, direction , time-tol , expr-tol , enable )
```

where *expression* is the required and *direction, time-tol, expr-tol,* and *enable* are optional arguments. The *expression, direction,* and *enable* arguments are specified as variable expressions. The tolerances (*time-tol* and *expr-tol*) are specified as constant expressions and shall be non-negative. Analog operators cannot be used for the *direction* or *enable* arguments and they should evaluate integers. If the tolerances are not specified, then the simulator sets them. If either or both tolerances are defined, then the direction shall also be defined.

If the direction indicator *direction* is set to 0 or is not specified, the cross() function event and time step control occur on both positive and negative crossings of the signal. If *direction* is +1 or -1, the event and time step control occur on rising or falling edge transitions of the signal, respectively, as shown in Figure 15-1. For any other values of *direction*, the cross() function does not generate an event and does not act to control the time step.

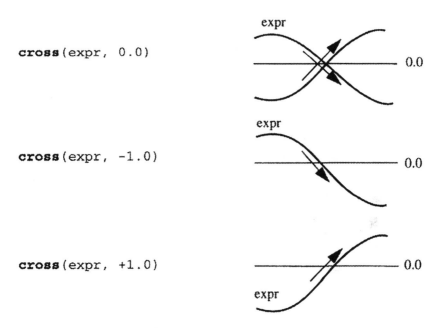

Figure 15-1. *Illustration of different specifications of the direction argument in the* cross() *monitored event function*

The *expr-tol* and *time-tol* arguments are absolute tolerances that represent the maximum allowable error between the true crossing point and when the cross event actually triggers. The event shall occur after the threshold crossing and while the signal remains in the box defined by actual crossing and *expr-tol* and *time-tol*, as shown in Figure 15-2.

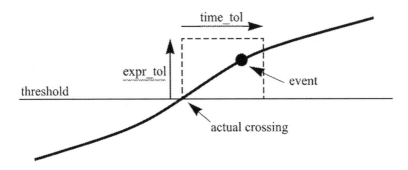

Figure 15-2. *Timing of event relative to threshold crossing*

If *expr-tol* is specified, *time-tol* shall also be specified and both tolerances shall be satisfied at the crossing.

If *enable* is specified and nonzero, then cross() behaves as just described. If the enable argument is specified and it is zero, then `cross()` is inactive, meaning that it does not generate an event at threshold crossings and does not act to control the time step. Thus, there are two ways to disable the `cross()` function, either by specifying enable as 0 or giving a value other than –1, 0, or 1 to dir.

The following example of a sample-and-hold module sah:

```
module sah (in, out, smpl);
  parameter real thresh = 0.0;
  parameter integer dir = +1 from [-1 : +1]
                                  exclude 0;
  output out;
  input in, smpl;
  electrical in, out, smpl;
  real state;
  analog begin
    @(cross(V(smpl) - thresh, dir))
      state = V(in);
    V(out) <+ transition(state, 0, 10n);
  end
endmodule
```

illustrates how the cross() function is used to set when the rising signal V(smpl) passes through a threshold value defined by parameter thresh.

Related to the cross() function is the last_crossing() function that returns a real value representing the simulation time when a signal expression last crossed zero.

Last Crossing Function

The syntax of the last crossing function is

```
last_crossing ( expression )
last_crossing ( expression , direction )
```

The optional *direction* argument shall evaluate to an integer expression +1, -1, or 0. If it is set to 0, the `last_crossing()` will return the most recent time the input expression had either a rising or falling edge transition. If the direction is +1 (-1), the `last_crossing()` will return the last time the input expression had a rising (falling) edge transition.

The `last_crossing()` function does not control the time step to get accurate results. It uses linear interpolation to estimate the time of the last crossing. It cannot be used as a monitoring event function. However, it can be used in combination with the event monitoring `cross()` function for improved accuracy. Before the *expression* crosses 0 for the first time, the `last_crossing()` function returns a negative value.

The following example measures the period of its input signal using the `cross()` and `last_crossing()` functions:

```
module period(in);
    input in;
    voltage in;
    integer crossings;
    real latest, previous;
    analog begin
      @(initial_step) begin
         crossings = 0;
         previous = 0;
      end
```

```
@(cross(V(in), +1)) begin
   crossings = crossings + 1;
   previous = latest;
end

latest = last_crossing(V(in), +1);

@(final_step) begin
if (crossings < 2)
    $strobe("Could not measure period.");
else
    $strobe("period = %g, crossings = %d",
    latest-previous, crossings);
end
   end
endmodule
```

In this way, the last_crossing() function benefits from the cross() function causing the simulator to place an evaluation point very near the threshold crossing. Together, they are considerably more accurate than either apart. And if the accuracy of the above is not sufficient, one can tighten the tolerances on the cross function.

Above Function

The above() function is almost identical to the cross() function, except that it also triggers during initialization or DC analysis. It generates a monitored event to detect threshold crossings when the expression crosses 0 from below. As with the cross() function, the above() function controls the time step to accurately resolve the crossing during transient analysis.

The above function is used in one of the syntax forms:

```
above ( expression )
above ( expression , time-tol )
above ( expression , time-tol , expr-tol )
above ( expression , time-tol , expr-tol , enable )
```

where *expression* is a required argument. The tolerances (*time-tol* and *expr-tol*) are optional arguments, but if specified shall be non-negative. All arguments are real expressions. If the tolerances are not specified, then the simulator sets them.

The above() function can generate an event during initialization. If the *expression* is positive after the initial condition analysis that precedes a transient analysis, the above() function shall generate an event. In contrast, the cross() function can only generate an event after the simulation time has advanced from zero. The cross() function will not generate events for non-transient analyses, such as AC, DC, or Noise analyses, but the above() function can. During a DC sweep, the above() function shall also generate an event when the expression crosses zero from below. However, the step size of the DC sweep is not controlled to accurately resolve the crossing.

If *enable* is specified and nonzero, then the above() function behaves as just described. If the enable argument is specified and it is zero, then above() is inactive, meaning that it does not generate an event at threshold crossings and does not act to control the time step.

The above() function maintains its internal state and has the same restrictions on its use as the cross() function.

Timer Function

The timer monitored event function is used to detect specific points in time. It can take one of the syntax forms:

```
timer ( start-time )
timer ( start-time ,  period )
timer ( start-time ,  period , time-tol )
timer ( start-time ,  period , time-tol , enable )
```

where *start-time* is the required and *period, time-tol,* and *enable* are optional arguments. The *start-time* and *period* arguments shall be expressions. The tolerance (*time-tol*) is a constant expression and shall be non-negative.

The timer() function schedules an event that occurs at an absolute time (*start-time*). If the period is specified and is greater than zero, the timer function schedules subsequent events at multiples of the *period* from the *start-time* as shown in Figure 15-3.

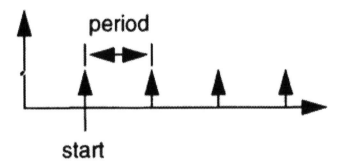

***Figure 15-3.** The schematic representation of events triggered by the* timer() *monitoring event function*

If the period expression evaluates to a value less than or equal to 0.0, the timer shall trigger only once at the specified *start-time*. The simulator places a time point within the *time-tol* of an event. If *time-tol* is not specified, the default time point is at, or just beyond, the time of the event.

If the *start-time* or period expressions change value during the evaluation of the analog block, the next event will be scheduled based on the latest value of the *start-time* and period.

If enable is specified and nonzero, then timer() behaves as just described. If the *enable* argument is specified and it is zero, then timer() is inactive, meaning that it does not generate events as long as enable is zero. However, it will start generating events once *enable* returns to be nonzero as if they had never been disabled.

A pseudo-random bitstream generator:

```
module bitStream (out);
  output out;
  electrical out;
  parameter period = 1.0;
  integer x;
  analog begin
    @(timer(0, period))
      x = $random + 0.5;
      V(out) <+ transition( x, 0.0, period/100.0 );
  end
endmodule
```

is an example of how the timer function can be used.

CHAPTER 16

Runtime Support

This chapter introduces system functions for querying on elaboration status and simulation environments as well as system functions providing runtime support to the numerical solver and control of the simulation.

Elaboration Queries

Module ports need not be connected and module parameters may not be overridden when the module is instantiated. In some cases, the module evaluation could depend on the information of actual port connectivities and the status of the parameter override. Verilog-A provides system functions that can be used to query that information.

Port Connections

The $port_connected() function can be used to determine whether a connection was specified for a port. The $port_connected() function takes one argument, which must be a port identifier. The return value shall be 1 if the port was connected to a net (by order or by name) when the module was instantiated, and 0 otherwise.

Note   The port may be connected to a net that has no other connections, but $port_connected( ) shall still return 1.

© Slobodan Mijalković 2022
S. Mijalković, *A Practical Guide to Verilog-A*, https://doi.org/10.1007/978-1-4842-6351-8_16

In the following example:

```
if ($port_connected(vout))
    V(vout) <+ transition( q, tdel, trise, tfall);
else
    V(vout) <+ 0.0;
```

the $port_connected() function is used to skip the transition filter for unconnected port vout.

Parameter Overrides

In some cases, it is important to be able to determine whether a parameter value was obtained from the default value in its declaration statement or if that value was overridden. In such a case, the $param_given() function can be used to detect parameter override. The system function $param_given() takes a single argument, which must be a parameter identifier. The return value shall be 1 if the parameter was overridden, either by a defparam statement or by a module instance parameter value assignment, and 0 otherwise.

The following example sets the variable temp to represent the device temperature:

```
if ($param_given(tdevice))
    temp = tdevice + `P_CELSIUS0;
else
    temp = $temperature;
```

Note that $temperature is not a constant expression, so it cannot be used as the default value of the parameter tdevice.

Simulation Queries

Verilog-A provides system functions for querying the current analysis type and simulation kernel parameters or for dynamically probing output variables within sibling instances during simulation.

Analysis Type

The `analysis()` query function with the syntax

`analysis ( analysis-name, ... )`

takes one or more string arguments *analysis-name* and returns 1 if any of the arguments match the current analysis type. Otherwise, it returns 0.

There is no fixed set of analysis types. Each simulator can support its own set. However, simulators shall use the names listed in Table 16-1 to represent analyses that are similar to those provided by SPICE-like simulators. Any unsupported type names are assumed to not be a match.

Table 16-1. *Analysis types*

Analysis Name	Analysis Description
"ac"	Small-signal AC analysis
"dc"	Operating point or DC sweep analysis
"noise"	Noise analysis
"tran"	Transient analysis
"ic"	The initial condition analysis which precedes a transient analysis
"static"	Any equilibrium point calculation, including a DC analysis as well as those that precede another analysis, such as the DC analysis which precedes an AC or noise analysis, or the IC analysis which precedes a transient analysis
"nodeset"	The phase during an equilibrium point calculation where nodesets are forced

Verilog-A supports a single-point DC analysis and also a multipoint DC sweep analysis in which multiple DC points are computed over a sweep of parameter values. During a DC sweep analysis, the values of variables after the operating point analysis for one DC point shall be used as the starting values for those variables for the next DC point. However, variable values shall not be carried over between two independent DC sweep analyses (from the last DC point of one analysis to the first DC point of the next analysis). Variables shall be re-initialized to zero at the start of each new analysis.

An operating point analysis is done for each DC point in the sweep. A single-point DC analysis is the same as an operating point analysis. The analysis("dc") and analysis("static") query function calls shall return true for a single-point DC analysis and also for every DC point in a sweep analysis. The analysis("nodeset") function call shall return true only during the phase of an operating point analysis in which nodeset values are enforced; that phase may occur in a single-point DC analysis or the first point of a multipoint DC sweep analysis but does not occur for subsequent points of a DC sweep.

Note   The constant expressions in the indirect contribution equation shall not include the analysis( ) function with an argument that can result in different return values during a single analysis, such as the "ic" or "nodeset" arguments.

Using the analysis() function, it is possible to have a module behave differently depending on which analysis is being run. In the following example:

```
if (analysis("ic"))
    V(cap) <+ initial_value;
else
    I(cap) <+ ddt(C*V(cap));
```

initial values of the capacitor voltage are specified using the analysis() function and switch branches.

Kernel Parameters

Verilog-A adds a set of system functions called the analog kernel parameter functions. These functions return information about the current environment parameters as a real value.

$temperature does not take any input arguments and returns the circuit's ambient temperature in Kelvin units.

$vt can optionally have a temperature (in Kelvin units) as an input argument and returns the thermal voltage (kT/q) at the given temperature. $vt without the optional input temperature argument returns the thermal voltage using $temperature.

$abstime returns the absolute time that is a real value number representing time in seconds.

$simparam function using a syntax

$simparam (*param-name*)
$simparam (*param-name, expression*)

queries the simulator for a real-valued simulation parameter named param_name. The argument *param-name* is a string value, either a string literal, string parameter, or a string variable. If *param-name* is known, its value is returned. If *param-name* is not known, and the optional expression is not supplied, then an error is generated. If the optional *expression* is supplied, its value is returned if param_name is not known and no error is generated. $simparam() shall always return a real value; simulation parameters that have integer values shall be coerced to real. There is no fixed list of simulation parameters. However, simulators shall accept the strings in Table 16-2 to access commonly known simulation parameters, if they support the parameter. Simulators can also accept other strings to access the same parameters.

Table 16-2. *Simulation real and integer parameter names*

String	Units	Description
gdev	1/Ohms	Additional conductance to be added to nonlinear branches for conductance homotopy convergence algorithm
gmin	1/Ohms	Minimum conductance placed in parallel with nonlinear branches
imax	Amps	Branch current threshold above which the constitutive relation of a nonlinear branch should be linearized

(continued)

Table 16-2. (*continued*)

String	Units	Description
imelt	Amps	Branch current threshold indicating device failure
iteration		Solver iteration number
scale		Scale factor for device instance geometry parameters
shrink		Optical linear shrink factor
simulatorSubversion		Simulator subversion
simulatorVersion		Simulator version
sourceScalefactor		Multiplicative factor for independent sources for source stepping homotopy convergence algorithm
tnom	Celsius	Default value of temperature at which model parameters were extracted

The values returned by simulatorVersion and simulatorSubversion are at the vendor's discretion, but the values shall be monotonically increasing for new versions or releases of the simulator, to facilitate checking that the simulator supports features that were added in a certain version of subversion.

In this first example, the variable gmin is set to the simulator's parameter named gmin, if it exists; otherwise, an error is generated.

```
gmin = $simparam("gmin");
```

In this second example, the variable sourcescale is set to the simulator's parameter sourceScaleFactor, if it exists; otherwise, the value 1.0 is returned.

```
sourcescale = $simparam("sourceScaleFactor", 1.0);
```

235

$simparam$str is similar to $simparam. However, it is used for returning string-valued simulation parameters. Table 16-3 gives a list of simulation string parameter names that shall be supported by $simparam$str.

Table 16-3. *Simulation string parameter names*

Parameter Name	Description
analysis_name	The name of the current analysis, e.g., tran1, mydc
analysis_type	The type of the current analysis, e.g., dc, tran, ac
cwd	The current working directory in which the simulator was started
module	The name of the module from which $simparam$str is called
instance	The hierarchical name of the instance from which $simparam$str is called
path	The hierarchical path to the $simparam$str function

Dynamic Probing

Verilog-A supports a system function that allows the probing of values within a sibling instance during simulation.

```
$simprobe( inst-name, param-name )
$simprobe( inst-name, param-name , expression )
```

$simprobe() queries the simulator for an output variable named *param-name* in a sibling instance called *inst-name*. The arguments *inst-name* and *param-name* are string values, either a string literal, string parameter, or a string variable.

To resolve the value, the simulator will look for an instance called *inst-name* in the parent of the current instance, that is, a sibling of the instance containing the $simprobe() expression. Once the instance is resolved, it will then query that instance for an output variable called *param_name*. If either the *inst-name* or *param-name* cannot be resolved, and the optional expression is not supplied, then an error shall be generated. If the optional expression is supplied, its value will be returned instead of raising an error. The intended use of this function is to allow dynamic monitoring of instance quantities.

```
module monitor;
    parameter string inst = "default";
    parameter string quant = "default";
    parameter real threshold = 0.0;
    real probe;
    analog begin
        probe = $simprobe(inst,quant);
        if (probe > threshold) begin
            $strobe("ERROR: Time %e:
                %s#%s (%g) > threshold (%e)",
                $abstime, inst, quant,
                probe, threshold);
            $finish;
        end
    end
endmodule
```

The module monitor will probe the quant in the instance inst. If its value becomes larger than the threshold, then the simulation will raise an error and stop.

```
module top(d,g,s);
    electrical d,g,s;
    inout d,g,s;
```

```
electrical gnd;
ground gnd;

SPICE_pmos#(.w(4u),.l(0.1u),.ad(4p),.as(4p),
           .pd(10u),.ps(10u))
mp(d,g,s,s);
SPICE_nmos #(.w(2u),.l(0.1u),.ad(2p),.as(2p),
            .pd(6u),.ps(6u)) mn(d,g,gnd,gnd);
monitor #(.inst("mn"), .quant("id"),
          .threshold(4.0e-3)) amonitor();
endmodule
```

Here, the monitor instance amonitor will keep track of the dynamic quantity id in the mosfet instance mn. If the value of id goes above the specified threshold of 4.0e-3 amps, then the instance amonitor will generate the error message and stop the simulation.

Solver Support

Verilog-A provides tasks and functions to support the nonlinear solver during simulation.

Announcing Discontinuity

The $discontinuity task is used to give hints to the simulator about the behavior of the module so the simulator can control its simulation algorithms to get accurate results in exceptional situations. This task does not directly specify the behavior of the module. $discontinuity shall be executed whenever the signal behavior changes discontinuously. The general form is

```
$discontinuity ;
$discontinuity ( constant-expression ) ;
```

where *constant-expression* indicates the degree of the discontinuity if the argument to $discontinuity is non-negative, that is, $discontinuity(i) implies a discontinuity in the ith derivative of the constitutive equation with respect to either a signal value or time where i must be a non-negative integer. Hence, $discontinuity(0) indicates a discontinuity in the equation, $discontinuity(1) indicates a discontinuity in its slope, etc. A special form of the $discontinuity task, $discontinuity(-1), is used with the $limit() function so -1 is also a valid argument of $discontinuity. Because discontinuous behavior can cause convergence problems, discontinuity shall be avoided whenever possible.

The filters (transition(), slew(), laplace(), etc.) can be used to smooth discontinuous behavior. However, in some cases, it is not possible to implement the desired functionality using these filters. In those cases, the $discontinuity task shall be executed when the signal behavior changes abruptly. Discontinuity created by switch branches and filters, such as transition() and slew(), does not need to be announced. The following example uses the discontinuity task to model a relay:

```
module relay (c1, c2, pin, nin) ;
    inout c1, c2;
    input pin, nin ;
    electrical c1, c2, pin, nin;
    parameter real r=1;
    analog begin
        @(cross(V(pin,nin))) $discontinuity;
        if (V(pin,nin) >= 0)
            I(c1,c2) <+ V(c1,c2)/r;
        else
            I(c1,c2) <+ 0 ;
    end
endmodule
```

In this example, cross() controls the time step so the time when the relay changes position is accurately resolved. It also triggers the $discontinuity task, which causes the simulator to react properly to the discontinuity. This would have been handled automatically if the type of the branch (c1,c2) had been switched between voltage and current.

Another example is a source that generates a triangular wave. In this case, neither the model nor the waveforms generated by the model are discontinuous. Rather, the waveform generated is piecewise linear with a discontinuous slope.

```
module triangle(out);
    output out;
    voltage out;
    parameter real period = 10.0, amplitude = 1.0;
    integer slope; real offset;

    analog begin
        @(timer(0, period)) begin
            slope = +1;
            offset = $abstime ;
            $discontinuity;
        end

        @(timer(period/2, period)) begin
            slope = -1 ;
            offset = $abstime;
            $discontinuity;
        end

        V(out) <+ amplitude*slope*
            (4*($abstime - offset)/period - 1);
    end
endmodule
```

If the simulator is aware of the abrupt change in slope, it can adapt to eliminate problems resulting from the discontinuous slope (typically changing to a first-order integration method).

Bounding Time Step

The $bound_step() task puts a bound on the next time step. It does not specify exactly what the next time step is, but it bounds how far the next time point can be from the present time point. The task takes the maximum time step as an argument. It does not return a value. The general form is

```
$bound_step ( expression );
```

where expression is a required argument and represents the maximum time step the simulator can advance. The expression argument shall be non-negative. If the value is less than the simulator's minimum allowable time step, the simulator's minimum time step shall be used instead. Refer to the simulator's documentation for further information regarding limits on step size for time-dependent analysis.

For a given time step, the simulator shall ensure that the next time step taken is no larger than the smallest $bound_step() argument currently active. The $bound_step() statement shall be ignored during a non-time-domain analysis.

The following example implements a sinusoidal voltage source and uses the $bound_step() task to assure the simulator faithfully follows the output signal:

```
module vsine(out);
    output out;
    voltage out;
    parameter real freq=1.0, ampl=1.0, offset=0.0;
```

```
    analog begin
        V(out) <+ ampl*sin(2.0*`M_PI*freq*$abstime)
                   + offset;
        $bound_step(0.05/freq);
    end
endmodule
```

It is forcing 20 points per cycle.

Limiting Iteration Steps

The $limit() function provides a method to indicate nonlinearities to the simulator and, if necessary, recommends a function to use to limit the change of its output from iteration to iteration. The general form is

```
$limit( access-function )
$limit( access-function ,analog-function-identifier )
$limit( access-function ,analog-function-identifier ,arg-list )
```

When the simulator has converged, the return value of the $limit() function is the value of the *access-function*, within appropriate tolerances. For some analysis types or solution methods, such as damped Newton-Raphson, the return value of the $limit() function may depend on the value of the access function and the internal state of the function. In all cases, the simulator is responsible for determining if limiting should be applied and what the return value is on a given iteration.

When more than one argument is supplied to the $limit() function, the second argument recommends a function to use to compute the return value. When the second argument is a string, it refers to a built-in function of the simulator. The two most common such functions are *pnjlim* and *fetlim*, which are found in SPICE and many SPICE-like simulators. Simulators may support other built-in functions and need not support *pnjlim* or *fetlim*. If the string refers to an unknown or unsupported function, the simulator is responsible for determining the appropriate limiting algorithm, just as if no string had been supplied.

pnjlim is intended for limiting arguments to exponentials, and the limexp() function may be implemented through a function derived from *pnjlim*. Two additional arguments to the $limit() function are required when the second argument to the limit function is the string "pnjlim": the third argument to $limit() indicates a step size *vte* and the fourth argument is a critical voltage *vcrit*. The step size *vte* is usually the product of the thermal voltage $vt and the emission coefficient of the junction.

fetlim is intended for limiting the potential across the oxide of a MOS transistor. One additional argument to the $limit() function is required when the second argument to the limit function is the string "fetlim": the third argument to $limit() is generally the threshold voltage of the MOS transistor.

In the case that none of the built-in functions of the simulator is appropriate for limiting the potential (or flow) used in a nonlinear equation, the second argument of the $limit() function may be an identifier referring to a user-defined function. In this case, if the simulator determines that limiting is needed to improve convergence, it will pass the two quantities as arguments to the user-defined function. The first argument of the user-defined function shall be the value of the access function reference for the current iteration. The second argument shall be the appropriate internal state; generally, this is the value that was returned by the $limit() function on the previous iteration. If more than two arguments are given to the $limit() function, then the third and subsequent arguments are passed as the third and subsequent arguments of the user-defined function. The arguments of the user-defined function shall all be declared input.

In order to prevent convergence when the output of the $limit() function is not sufficiently close to the value of the access function reference, the user-defined function shall call $discontinuity(-1) when its return value is not sufficiently close to the value of its first argument.

The following module defines a diode and includes an analog function that mimics the behavior of *pnjlim* in SPICE. Though limexp() could have been used for the exponential in the current, using $limit() allows the same voltage to be used in the charge calculation.

```
module diode(a,c);
  inout a, c;
  electrical a, c;
  parameter real IS = 1.0e-14;
  parameter real CJO = 0.0;

  analog function real spicepnjlim;
    input vnew, vold, vt, vcrit;
    real vnew, vold, vt, vcrit, vlimit, arg;
    begin
      vlimit=vnew;
      if ((vnew > vcrit) &&
          (abs(vnew-vold) > (vt+vt)))
        begin
         if (vold > 0) begin
           arg = 1 + (vnew-vold) / vt;
           if (arg > 0)
             vlimit = vold + vt * ln(arg);
           else
             vlimit = vcrit;
         end
      else
```

```
      vlimit = vt * ln(vnew/vt);
      $discontinuity(-1);
    end
    spicepnjlim = vlimit;
  end
endfunction

  real vdio, idio, qdio, vcrit;
  analog begin
    vcrit=0.7;
    vdio = $limit(V(a,c), spicepnjlim, $vt, vcrit);
    idio = IS * (exp(vdio/$vt) - 1);
    I(a,c) <+ idio;
    if (vdio < 0.5) begin
      qdio = 0.5 * CJ0 * (1-sqrt(1-V(a,c)));
    end else begin
      qdio = CJ0* (2.0*(1.0-sqrt(0.5)) +
             sqrt(2.0)/2.0*(vdio*vdio+vdio-3.0/4.0));
    end
    I(a,c) <+ ddt(qdio);
  end
endmodule
```

The limexp() function is an analog operator whose internal state contains information about the argument on previous iterations. The general form is

limexp(*expr*)

It returns a real value which is the exponential of its single real argument, and its apparent behavior is not distinguishable from exp(). However, limexp() internally limits the change of its output from iteration to iteration in order to improve convergence. On any iteration where the change in the output of the limexp() function is bounded, the simulator is prevented from terminating the iteration. Thus, the simulator can only converge when the output of limexp() equals the exponential of the input.

Simulation Control

Verilog-A provides system functions for announcing severity and terminating simulation.

Announcing Severity

The fatal system severity task

```
$fatal ;
$fatal ( finish_number ) ;
$fatal ( finish_number, message-argument, ...  ) ;
```

The severity task $fatal shall generate a runtime fatal assertion error, which terminates the simulation with an error code. $fatal terminates the simulation without checking whether the iteration would be rejected. If $fatal is executed within an analog initial block, then after outputting the message, the initialization may be aborted, and in no case shall simulation proceed past initialization. Some of the system severity task calls may not be executed either.

Calling $fatal results in an implicit call to $finish that terminates the simulation. The first argument, *finish-number*, passed to $fatal shall be consistent with the corresponding argument to the $finish system task, which sets the level of diagnostic information reported by the tool. The *finish-number* may be used in an implementation-specific manner.

Non-fatal system severity tasks

```
severity-task ;
severity-task ();
```

severity-task (*message-argument, ...*   ) ;

where the *severity-task* is one of the system tasks:

$error $warning $info

The $error shall be a runtime error. $warning shall be a runtime warning, which can be suppressed in a tool-specific manner. $info shall indicate that the assertion failure carries no specific severity.

Non-fatal system severity tasks called during a rejected iteration shall have no effect. If $error is executed within an analog initial block, then the message is issued and the initialization continues. However, the simulation shall not proceed past initialization. The other two tasks, $warning and $info, only output their text message but do not affect the rest of the initialization and the simulation.

For simulation tools, these tasks shall also report the simulation runtime at which the severity system task is called. If any of these tasks is called during a DC sweep, the simulator shall report the current value of the swept variable in place of the simulation runtime. If the task is called from an analog initial block, the simulator shall report that the call was made during initialization.

Each of these system tasks can also include additional user-specified information using the same format as the $display function.

Terminating Simulation

Verilog-A provides two simulation control tasks to terminate simulation, $finish and $stop. The syntax for the $finish task is:

$finish ;
$finish (*level*);

If $finish is called during an accepted iteration, then the simulator shall exit after the current solution is complete. $finish called during a rejected iteration shall have no effect. As a result of the simulation terminating due to a $finish task, it is expected that all appropriate final_step blocks are also triggered. If $finish is called from an analog initial block, the simulator shall exit without performing the simulation. If $finish is called from within an analog initial block, the simulator shall report that the call was made during initialization in place of the simulation time. If $finish is called from the analog context during a DC sweep (but outside of an analog initial block), the simulator shall report the current value of the swept variable in place of the simulation time.

The syntax for the $stop task is:

```
$stop ;
$stop ( level );
```

A call to $stop during an accepted iteration causes simulation to be suspended at a converged time point. The $stop task shall not be used within an analog initial block. The mechanism for resuming simulation is left to the implementation.

Table 16-4. *Diagnostic messages*

Level	Message
0	Prints nothing
1	Prints simulation time and location (default)
2	Prints simulation time, location, and statistics about the memory and CPU time used in the simulation

The $finish and $stop tasks take an optional expression argument, which determines what type of diagnostic message is printed. The amount of diagnostic message output increases with the value of n as shown in Table 16-4. The *level* value 1 is the default if no argument, or an argument different than 0, 1, or 2 is supplied.

CHAPTER 17

Input and Output

In this chapter, we look into Verilog-A functions and tasks for the display of data on the console or writing to and reading data from files. Even though your simulator will let you monitor the value of signals and variables in your design, it is also nice to be able to output certain information beyond the simulator reporting capabilities. This is useful when the results of a simulation are large and need to be stored in a file or when data is to be read from an external file and driven into a model formulation.

File Management

Verilog-A provides various tasks and functions to deal with files. It includes opening files, positioning files for reading and writing, detecting error status and end of the files, and finally closing files.

Opening Files

The files are opened and closed using $fopen and $fclose system functions following the syntax:

```
mcd-or-fd = $fopen( file-name );
mcd-or-fd = $fopen( file-name , type );
```

© Slobodan Mijalković 2022
S. Mijalković, *A Practical Guide to Verilog-A*, https://doi.org/10.1007/978-1-4842-6351-8_17

The $fopen function opens the file specified with the *file-name* argument. The *file-name* argument shall be a string literal, string data type, or an integer number containing a character string that names the file to be opened. The optional *type* argument shall be a string expression that evaluates one of the strings given in Table 17-1.

Table 17-1. *The values of the type file descriptors*

Type Argument	Description
"r" or "rb"	Open for reading
"w" or "wb"	Truncate to zero length or create for writing
"a" or "ab"	Append; open for writing at end-of-file, or create for writing
"r+", "r+b", or "rb+"	Open for update (reading and writing)
"w+", "w+b", or "wb+"	Truncate or create for update
"a+", "a+b", or "ab+"	Append; open or create for update at end-of-file

The *type* argument indicates how the file should be opened. If *type* is omitted, the file is opened for writing, and a multichannel descriptor *mcd* is returned. If *type* is supplied, the file is opened as specified by the value of the *type* string. The "b" in the *type* strings exists to distinguish binary files from text files. Many operating systems (such as Unix) make no distinction between binary and text files, and on these systems, the "b" is ignored. However, some systems (such as machines running Windows) perform data mappings on certain binary values written to and read from files that are opened for text access.

Note   Verilog-A supports multiple analyses during the same simulation process. If a file is opened in a write mode in the first analysis and reopened in that write mode in the following analysis, then content written from the following analyses shall be appended to the content written during the previous analyses.

When called, the $fopen task returns a 32-bit integer *mcd-or-fd* which is either a multichannel descriptor, *mcd*, or a file descriptor, *fd*, determined by the absence or presence of the *type* argument in the $fopen function call. If a file cannot be opened (either the file does not exist and the type specified is "r", "rb", "r+", "r+b", or "rb+", or the permissions do not allow the file to be opened at that path), zero is returned for the *mcd-or-fd*. Applications can call the $ferror function to determine the cause of the most recent error.

In the multichannel descriptor *mcd*, a single bit is set indicating which file is opened. The least significant bit (bit 0) of *mcd* always refers to the standard output. The output is directed to two or more files opened with multichannel descriptors by bitwise OR-ing together their multichannel descriptors and writing to the resulting value. The most significant bit (bit 31) of a multichannel descriptor is reserved and shall always be cleared, limiting an implementation to at most 31 files opened for output via multichannel descriptors.

Note   The number of simultaneous input and output channels that can be opened at any one time is dependent on the operating system.

The most significant bit (bit 31) of *fd* is reserved and shall always be set; this allows implementations of the file input and output functions to determine how the file was opened. The remaining bits hold a small number indicating what file is opened. Three file descriptors are pre-opened; they are STDIN, STDOUT, and STDERR, which have the values 32'h8000_0000, 32'h8000_0001, and 32'h8000_0002, respectively. STDIN is pre-opened for reading, and STDOUT and STDERR are pre-opened for append. Unlike multichannel descriptors, file descriptors cannot be combined via bitwise OR to direct output to multiple files. Instead, files are opened via file descriptor for input, output, and both input and output, as well as for append operations, based on the value of *type*, according to Table 17-1.

File Positioning

The three system functions can be used to get files positioned for data input and output.

The function $ftell() used with the syntax:

offset = $ftell (*fd*);

tells you where you are in the file *fd* by returning the byte number of the next byte which will be read or written in a file. The *offset* number is always relative to the beginning of the file. If an error occurs, –1 is returned.

The $fseek() function used the syntax:

code = $fseek (*fd* , *offset* , *operation*);

repositions the file to a different location. The next byte to be read or written will be at the new position. The $fseek() function requires three arguments: the *fd* file descriptor; an offset number, which can be a positive or negative integer value; and an operation code *operation*. The code *operation* must be 0, 1, or 2, where

- 0 indicates that the file position should be set to the offset value.

- 1 indicates that the file position should be set to the current position plus the offset.

- 2 indicates that the file position should be set to the end-of-file plus the offset.

It is legal to set the file position to beyond the end of the file. The next write to the file will extend the file size to the new byte number, filling the gap with zeros. A file that is opened in append mode cannot be written to at a location before the end-of-file. If $fseek() sets the file position to another location, the location can be read, but the next write will automatically reposition the file position back to the current end-of-file.

The function $rewind() with the syntax

code = $rewind (*fd*);

repositions the file to the beginning of the file. It has the same effect as

code = $fseek (*fd* ,0   ,0);

If an error occurs repositioning the file, then the *code* is set to –1. Otherwise, the *code* is set to 0. Applications can call $ferror to determine the cause of the most recent error.

If a file is being read from during an iterative solve and if that iteration is rejected, then the file pointer is reset to the file position that it pointed to before the iterative solve started. The features of the underlying implementation of file input-output (I/O) on the host system may prevent the file position from being reset after an iteration is rejected. In this case, a fatal error will be reported.

Error Status

Should any error be detected by one of the file input and output routines, an error code is returned. Often, this is sufficient for normal operation (i.e., if the opening of an optional configuration file fails, the application typically would simply continue using default values). However, sometimes it is useful to obtain more information about the error for correct application operation. In this case, the $ferror function can be used. It has a syntax:

errno = $ferror (*fd*, *str*);

   The arguments supplied to the $ferror() function are a file *fd* and string *str* which should be at least 640 bits wide. The description of the type of error encountered by the most recent file I/O operation is written into *str*. The integral value of the error code is returned in *errno*. If the most recent operation did not result in an error, then the value returned shall be zero, and the string variable *str* shall be empty.

Detecting End-of-File

The function $feof() with the syntax

code = $feof (*fd*);

   is used to detect end-of-file. It returns a nonzero value when end-of-file has previously been detected reading the input file *fd*. It returns zero otherwise.

Flushing Output

The system task $fflush() with the syntax

```
$fflush ( mcd );
$fflush ( fd );
$fflush ( );
```

writes any buffered output to the file(s) specified by *mcd* or *fd*, or if $fflush is invoked with no arguments, to all open files.

Closing Files

The files are closed using $fclose system tasks following the syntax:

```
$fclose( mcd-or-fd );
```

The $fclose system task closes the file specified by *fd* or closes the file(s) specified by the multichannel descriptor *mcd*. No further output to or input from any file descriptor(s) closed by $fclose is allowed. The $fopen function shall reuse channels that have been closed.

Reading Data

Verilog-A provides the ability to read values from files and load them into variables. Files opened using file descriptors (*fd*) can be read-only if they were opened with either the r or r+ type values.

Reading a Line from a File

One line can be read from a file using the $fgets system function. It is based on the C language standard library function fgets. The syntax is

```
number-of-characters-read = $fgets ( str, fd )
```

where *fd* is a 32-bit integer file descriptor and *str* is the name of the string variable.

The system function $fgets reads characters from the file specified by *fd* into the string variable *str* until it is filled, the newline character is read, or the end-of-file is reached, whichever comes first. The $fgets function returns the number of characters read. If an error occurs reading from the file, then the return value is set to zero. Applications can call $ferror() to determine the cause of the most recent error.

Reading Formatted Data

The $fscanf and $sscanf system functions can be used to format data as it is read from a file. The syntax is

```
number-of-args-assigned = $fscanf ( fd , format , arg , ... )
number-of-args-assigned = $sscanf ( str , format , arg , ... )
```

$fscanf reads from the files specified by the file descriptor *fd*, while $sscanf reads from the string *str*. The string *str* shall be a string variable, string parameter, or a string literal. Both functions read characters, interpret them according to a specified format, and store the results. Both $fscanf and $sscanf system functions expect as arguments a control string, *format*, and a set of arguments specifying where to place the results.

The arguments must be variables of the appropriate data type for the format code. If there are insufficient arguments for the format, the behavior is undefined. If the format is exhausted while arguments remain, the excess arguments are ignored. If an argument is too small to hold the converted input, then, in general, the least significant bits are transferred. Arguments of any length that is supported by Verilog-A can be used. However, if the destination is real, then the value +inf (or -inf) is transferred.

The *format* is a `string` data type or a string expression. The string contains conversion specifications, which direct the conversion of input into the arguments. The control string can contain the following:

- Whitespace characters (blanks, tabs, newlines, or formfeeds) that cause input to be read up to the next non-whitespace character. For `$sscanf`, null characters shall also be considered whitespace.

- An ordinary character (not %) that must match the next character of the input stream.

- Conversion specifications consist of the character %, an optional assignment suppression character *, a decimal digit string that specifies an optional numerical maximum field width, and a conversion code.

A conversion specification directs the conversion of the next input field. The result is placed in the variable specified in the corresponding argument unless assignment suppression was indicated by the character *. In this case, no argument shall be supplied. For example:

```
n = $fscanf(fd, "%t %d", r, i);
n = $fscanf(fd, "%t,%d", r, i);
n = $fscanf(fd, "%t*%d", r, i);
```

demonstrate format strings for reading values separated by a whitespace, comma, and any character.

The suppression of assignment provides a way of describing an input field that is to be skipped. An input field is defined as a string of nonspace characters; it extends to the next inappropriate character or until the maximum field width, if one is specified, is exhausted. For all descriptors except the character c, whitespace leading an input field is ignored. Table 17-2 describes the input field characters.

Table 17-2. *Input field characters*

Descriptor	Description
%	A single % is expected in the input at this point; no assignment is done
d	Matches an optionally signed decimal number, consisting of the optional sign from the set + or −, followed by a sequence of characters from the set 0,1,2,3,4,5,6,7,8,9, and _
f, e, or g	Matches a floating-point number. The format of a floating-point number is an optional sign (either + or −), followed by a string of digits from the set 0,1,2,3,4,5,6,7,8,9 optionally containing a decimal point character (.), followed by an optional exponent part including e or E, followed by an optional sign, followed by a string of digits from the set 0,1,2,3,4,5,6,7,8,9
r	Matches a real number in engineering notation, using the scale factors defined in
s	Matches a string, which is a sequence of non-whitespace characters
m	Returns the current hierarchical path as a string. Do not read data from the input file or str argument

If an invalid conversion character follows the %, the results of the operation are implementation dependent. If the end-of-file is encountered during input, conversion is terminated. If the end-of-file occurs before any characters matching the current directive have been read (other than leading whitespace, where permitted), the execution of the current directive terminates with an input failure. Otherwise, unless the execution of the current directive is terminated with a matching failure, the execution of the following directive (if any) is terminated with an input failure.

If conversion terminates on a conflicting input character, the offending input character is left unread in the input stream. Trailing whitespace (including newline characters) is left unread unless matched by a directive. The success of literal matches and suppressed assignments is not directly determinable.

$fscanf and $fscanf return the number of successfully matched and assigned input arguments. This number can be 0 in the event of an early matching failure between an input character and the control string. If the input ends before the first matching failure or conversion, the end-of-file is returned. Applications can call $ferror to determine the cause of the most recent error.

Displaying and Writing Data

Verilog-A provides system tasks for displaying and writing data as text output, file output, and writing data to strings.

Text Output

Text output system tasks are used to print strings and variable values to the console or transcript of a simulation tool. The text output system tasks have a syntax:

```
text-output-task ( );
text-output-task ( arg1, ... );
```

where the *text-output-task* is one of the system tasks:

```
$display $write $strobe $monitor $debug
```

Text output system tasks display a list of arguments to the console or transcript of a simulation tool. The arguments are displayed in the same order as they appear in the argument list. Each argument can be a quoted string literal, an expression that returns a value, or a null argument. A null argument is characterized by two adjacent commas (, ,) in the argument list. Any null argument produces a single space character in the display output. If the display system task is invoked without arguments, it simply prints a newline character.

All the text output tasks, except $debug, shall not display output unless an iteration has been accepted. The $debug task provides the capability to display simulation data while the analog simulator is solving the equations. The $debug system task outputs its arguments for each iteration of the analog solver even if the evaluation occurred during an iteration that was rejected. The only difference between $display and $write is that $display appends a newline after printing the arguments and $write does not. $strobe is the same as $display, but printing occurs after the simulator has converged on a solution for all nodes.

The $monitor task provides the ability to display the values of any variables or expressions specified as arguments to the task only if their values change. When a $monitor task is invoked with one or more arguments, the simulator sets up a mechanism whereby for each accepted iteration step, if the variable or an expression in the argument list changes value compared with the last accepted step, except for the $abstime or $realtime system functions, the entire argument list is displayed at the end of the time step as if reported by the $strobe task. If two or more arguments change the value at the same time, only one display is produced that shows the new values.

File Output

Each of the text output system tasks has a counterpart in the file output system tasks, which write to specific files. The syntax is

```
file-output-task ( mcd-or-fd );
file-output-task ( mcd-or-fd , arg1 , ... );
```

The *file-output-task* is one of the system tasks:

```
$fdisplay $fwrite $fstrobe $fmonitor $fdebug
```

These counterpart system tasks accept the same type of arguments as the tasks upon which they are based, with one exception: the first argument shall be either a multichannel descriptor or a file descriptor, which indicates where to direct the file output. A multichannel descriptor is either a variable or the result of an expression that takes the form of a 32-bit unsigned integer value. The file output system tasks work just like their counterparts, except that they write to files using the file descriptor.

An example of using text and file output system tasks to multiple files is the following module:

```
module f2;
  integer file1, file2;
  initial begin
    file1 = $fopen("file1");
    file2 = $fopen("file2");
    $display("The number used for file 1 is %0d",
             file1);
    $display("The number used for file 2 is %0d",
             file2);
    $fdisplay(file1, "Hello File 1");
    $fdisplay(file2, "Hello File 2");
    $fdisplay(file1 file2, "Hello both files");
    $fdisplay(file1 file2 | 1,
              "Hello files and screen");
    $fdisplay(file1, "Good Bye File 1");
    $fdisplay(file2, "Good Bye File 2");
    $fclose(file1);
    $fclose(file2);
  end
endmodule
```

Writing Data to a String

The system tasks for writing and formatting data to a string have a syntax:

```
$swrite ( str );
$swrite ( str , arg1, ... );
$sformat ( str, format );
$sformat ( str, format , arg1, ... );
```

The $swrite system task is based on the $fwrite system task and accepts the same type of arguments with one exception. The first argument to $swrite shall be a string variable to which the data shall be written, instead of a variable specifying the file to which to write the resulting string.

The system task $sformat is similar to the system task $swrite, with one major difference. Unlike the text and file output system tasks, $sformat always interprets its second argument, and only its second argument, as a format string. This format argument can be a static string, such as "data is %d", or can be a string variable whose content is interpreted as the format string. No other arguments are interpreted as format strings. $sformat supports all the format specifiers supported by the file output system tasks. The remaining arguments to $sformat are processed using any format specifiers in the *format* until all such format specifiers are used up. If not enough arguments are supplied for the format specifiers or too many are supplied, then the application shall issue a warning and continue execution. The application, if possible, can statically determine a mismatch in format specifiers and number of arguments and issue a compile-time error message. If the *format* is a string variable, it might not be possible to determine its value at compile time.

Escape Sequences

The contents of string arguments are output literally, except when certain escape sequences are inserted to display special characters or specify the display format for subsequent expressions. The escape sequences are shown in Table 17-3.

Table 17-3. *Escape sequences for printing special characters*

Escape Sequence	Special Character
\n	The newline character
\t	The tab character
\\	The \ character
\"	The " character
\ddd	A character specified by 1 to 3 octal digits
%%	The % character

For example:

```
$display("\\\t\\\n\"\123");
```

produces at the output:

```
\      \
"S
```

Table 17-4 shows the escape sequences used for format specifications. The special character % indicates that the next character should be interpreted as a format specification that establishes the display format for a subsequent expression argument. For each % character (except %m, %%, and %1) that appears in a string, a corresponding expression argument shall be supplied after the string.

Table 17-4. *Escape sequences for format specification*

Escape Sequence	Display Format
%h or %H	Display in hexadecimal format
%d or %D	Display in decimal format
%o or %O	Display in octal format
%b or %B	Display in binary format
%c or %C	Display in ASCII character format
%1 or %L	Display library binding information
%m or %M	Display hierarchical name
%s or %S	Display as a string

The formatting specification %1 (or %L) is defined for displaying the library information of the specific module. The %m format specifier does not accept an argument. Instead, it causes the display task to print the hierarchical name of the module, task, function, or named block which invokes the system task containing the format specifier. This is useful when there are many instances of the module which call the system task.

The %s format specifier is used to print ASCII codes as characters. For each %s specification which appears in a string, a corresponding argument shall follow the string in the argument list. The associated argument is interpreted as a sequence of 8-bit hexadecimal ASCII codes, with every 8 bits representing a single character. If the argument is a variable, its value shall be right-justified so the rightmost bit of the value is the least significant bit of the last character in the string. No termination character or value is required at the end of a string and leading zeros (0) are never printed.

The format specifications in Table 17-5 are used for real numbers and have the full formatting capabilities available in the C language. For example, the format specification %10.3g sets a minimum field width of 10 with three (3) fractional digits.

Table 17-5. *Format specifications for real numbers*

Escape Sequence	Displayed Format
%e or %E	Display real in an exponential format
%f or %F	Display real in a decimal format
%g or %G	Display real in exponential or decimal format, whichever format results in the shorter printed output
%r or %R	Display real in engineering notation, using the scale factors

Any expression argument which has no corresponding format specification is displayed using the default decimal format.

CHAPTER 18

Generative Programming

Generative programming is used to create conditional or multiple instances of modules, branches, functions, variables, nets, and other generable module items. This is a powerful tool for parameterizing and configuring the module's architecture and simplifying its implementation. It allows for modules with the repetitive structure to be described more concisely and also provides the ability for parameter values to affect the structure of Verilog-A models. Although the generate statements use syntax very similar to the procedural conditional and looping statements, it is important to recognize that they do not execute at simulation time. Generate statements are executed during the elaboration of the model which occurs after parsing and before simulation.

Generate Blocks

A generate block is a collection of one or more generable module items which could be conditionally or recursively instantiated using generate programming statements. A generate block is defined by the syntax

```
begin : block-name
      generable-module-item ...
end
```

© Slobodan Mijalković 2022
S. Mijalković, *A Practical Guide to Verilog-A*, https://doi.org/10.1007/978-1-4842-6351-8_18

The use of the identifier *block-name* is optional and generate blocks can be used unnamed:

```
begin
     generable-module-item ...
end
```

If a generate block consists of only one generable module item, it can be used without begin and end keywords:

```
generable-module-item
```

which is the simplest form of unnamed generate block.

Most of the Verilog-A module items can be recursively or conditionally instantiated by generate statements. It is perhaps simpler to mention which module items are not possible to instantiate via generative programming. The non-generable module items are port direction and type declaration statements and module-level parameter declarations (including parameter aliases). All other module items including the generative statements themselves are generable and can appear in the generate blocks.

The elaboration of a generate statement results in zero or more instances of a generable block. An instance of a generate block is similar in some ways to an instance of a module. It creates a new level of hierarchy. It brings the declared objects, analog constructs, and module instances within the generate block into existence. Names in instantiated named generable blocks can be referenced hierarchically.

It should be mentioned that, unlike the procedural block statements, generate blocks do not represent statements themselves. Generate blocks can be used only within generate statements.

Generate Statements

There are two kinds of statements that control generative instantiation: conditional and loop statements. The conditional generate statements instantiate only selected generable module items, while the loop generate statements allow recursive instantiation of generable module items. The generate statements could be defined within the module using generate regions.

Generate Regions

A generate region is a textual span in the module description where generate statements may appear. The syntax of the generate region is

generate *generate-statement* ...   endgenerate

where keywords generate and endgenerate define the scope of a generate region. Generate regions do not nest, and they may only occur directly within a module.

The explicit use of generate regions is optional. In principle, there is no semantic difference in the module when generative statements are introduced without defined generate regions. Generate regions are mainly used to improve the readability of the code by explicitly annotating the code segments containing generate statements.

Conditional Generation

The conditional *if-generate* and *case-generate* statements select at most one generate block from a set of alternative generate blocks based on constant conditional expressions evaluated during elaboration. The selected generate block, if any, is instantiated into the model. The syntax of the *if-generate* statement is

if (*const-expression*) *generate-block*

or the extended syntax with the else clause:

```
if ( const-expression )
     generate-block
else
     generate-block
```

The latter is also known as the generative if-else statement. The syntax of the *case-generate* statement is

```
case ( const-expression )
   case-item, ... : generate-block
   case-item, ... : generate-block
      ...
   default : generate-block
endcase
```

The syntax for conditional generate statements fully resembles that of procedural conditional statements. It is permissible to combine *if-generate* and *case-generate* statements in the same complex generate constructs. However, direct nesting applies only to conditional generative statements nested in conditional generative statements. It does not apply in any way to loop generative statements.

Because at most one of the alternative generate blocks is instantiated, it is permissible to have more than one block with the same name within a single conditional generate statement. However, it is not permissible for any of the named generate blocks to have the same name as generate blocks in any other conditional statements in the same scope, even if the blocks with the same name are not selected for instantiation. It is not permissible for any of the named generate blocks to have the same name as any other declaration in the same scope, even if that block is not selected for instantiation.

Conditional generate constructs make it possible for a module to contain an instantiation of itself. The same can be said of loop generate constructs, but it is more easily done with conditional generates. With proper use of parameters, the resulting recursion can be made to terminate, resulting in a legitimate model hierarchy. Because of the rules for determining top-level modules, a module containing an instantiation of itself will not be a top-level module.

The following example of nlres module implements a nonlinear resistor using an *if-generate* statement:

```
module nlres (inout electrical a,
              inout electrical b);
    parameter real res = 1k from (0:inf);
    parameter real coeff1 = 0.0;

    generate
        if ($param_given(coeff1) && coeff1 != 0.0)
            analog V(a, b) <+ res *
                (1.0 + coeff1 * I(a, b)) * I(a, b);
        else if (res == 0.0)
            analog V(a, b) <+ 0.0;
        else
            resistor #(.r(res)) R1(a, b);
    endgenerate
endmodule
```

The *if-generate* statement is used to select among the resistance contribution statement, the SPICE resistor primitive, or a short if the resistance value is 0.

For compact modeling of semiconductor devices, the introduction of extra nodes can be controlled with if-generate statements as shown in the module nmosfet:

```
module nmosfet (d, g, s, b);
    inout electrical d, g, s, b;
    parameter integer nqsMod = 0 from [0:1];

    if (nqsMod) begin : nqs
        electrical GP;
        electrical BP;
        electrical BI;
        electrical BS;
        electrical BD;
    end

    ...

endmodule
```

The internal electrical nodes GP, BP, BI, BS, and BD are created only if the nqsMod parameter has a nonzero value.

Looping Generation

The *for-generate* statement permits instantiating a generate block multiple times. The syntax of the *for-generate* statement is

```
for ( genvar-initialization ; genvar-control ; genvar-change )
    generate-block
```

Similar to the procedural for-loop statement, the *for-generate* statement employs three actions, *genvar-initialization*, *genvar-control*, and *genvar-change*, for the conditional instantiation of a *generate-block*. The main difference is that the *for-generate* statement actions are composed using a genvar index variable instead of an integer index variable used in procedural for-loops.

Genvars are integer-valued variables declared by the syntax

```
genvar genvar-name, ... ;
```

where the keyword genvar is followed by the list of identifiers *genvar-name*. A genvar variable is used as an integer index only during the elaboration of *for-generate* statements. It does not exist at simulation time and shall not be referenced anywhere other than in *for-generate* statements. Both the *genvar-initialization* and *genvar-change* assignments in the *for-generate* statement shall assign to the same genvar variable. Moreover, the *genvar-initialization* assignment shall not reference the genvar index variable on the right-hand side.

If the *generate-block* is named, the *for-generate* statement implicitly declares an array of block instances. The index values in this array are the values of the used genvar variable during elaboration. This can be a sparse array because the genvar values do not have to form a contiguous range of integers. The array is considered to be declared even if the *for-generate* statement produces no instances of the generate block.

If the *generate-block* is not named, the declarations within it cannot be referenced using hierarchical names other than from within the hierarchy instantiated by the generate block itself. It shall be an error if the name of a generate block instance array conflicts with any other declaration, including any other generate block instance array. It shall be an error if the *for-generate* statement does not terminate. It shall be an error if a genvar value is repeated during the evaluation of the *for-generate* statement. It implies some restriction on the usage of a defparam statement in a *generate-block*. It may not target a parameter in another instantiation of the same generate block, even when the other instantiation is created by the same loop generate construct. Similarly, a defparam statement in one instance of an array of generated instances may not target a parameter in another instance of the instance array.

Within a *generate-block* of a *for-generate* statement, there is an implicitly declared local parameter. This is an integer parameter that has the same name as genvar variable, and its value within each instance of the generated block is the value of genvar variable at the time the instance was elaborated. This parameter can be used anywhere within the generated block that a normal parameter with an integer value can be used. It can be referenced with a hierarchical name. Because this implicit local parameter has the same name as the genvar variable, any reference to this name inside the loop generate block will be a reference to the localparam, not to the genvar. As a consequence, it is not possible to have two nested loop generate constructs that use the same genvar variable.

The example of module genvarexp demonstrates the use of the genvar variable in the *for-generate* statement.

```
module genvarexp(out, dt);
    parameter integer width = 1;
    output out;
    input [1:width] dt;
    electrical out;
    electrical [1:width] dt;
    real tmp;

    genvar k;

    analog begin
       tmp = 0.0;
       for (k = 1; k <= width; k = k + 1) begin
             tmp = tmp + V(dt[k]);
             V(out) <+ ddt(V(dt[k]));
       end
       $strobe("Summ of potentials = %e", tmp);
    end
endmodule
```

Note that the *for-generate* statement is used here within the analog procedural block.

In the next example, the module `rcline` implements an interconnect line constructed from RC sections.

```
module rcline (n1, n2);
    inout n1, n2;
    electrical n1, n2, gnd; ground gnd;
    parameter integer N = 10 from (0:inf);
    electrical [0:N] n;
    parameter Cap = 1p, Res = 1k;
    localparam Csec = Cap/N, Rsec = Res/(2*N);

    genvar i;

    for (i=0; i<N; i=i+1) begin : section
        electrical n_int;
        resistor #(.r(Rsec)) R1(n[i], n_int);
        resistor #(.r(Rsec)) R2(n_int, n[i+1]);
        analog
            I(n_int, gnd) <+ Csec * ddt(V(n_int));
    end

    analog begin
        V(n1, n[0]) <+ 0.0;
        V(n2, n[N]) <+ 0.0;
    end
endmodule
```

The resistor network is generated by replicating the resistance module instances, while the capacitors are implemented by replicating a contribution statement in an analog block statement.

Hierarchy Scope and Names

Each instantiation of a generate block is considered to be a separate hierarchy scope. If the generate block selected for instantiation is named, then this name declares a generate block instance and is the name for the scope it creates. Normal rules for hierarchical naming apply. For each block instance created by the *for-generate* statements, the generate block identifier for the loop is indexed by adding the genvar value to the end of the generate block identifier. These names can be used in hierarchical path names.

If a generate block in a conditional generate statement consists of only one item, then this generate block is not treated as a separate scope, it is said to be directly nested. The directly nested generate blocks are treated as if they belong to the outer generate statement. Therefore, they can have the same name as the generate blocks of the outer generate statement, and they cannot have the same name as any declaration in the scope enclosing the outer generate statements (including other generate blocks in other generate constructs in that scope). This allows complex conditional generate schemes to be expressed without creating unnecessary levels of generate block hierarchy.

If the generate block selected for instantiation is not named, it still creates a scope, but the declarations within it cannot be referenced using hierarchical names. Although an unnamed generate block has no name that can be used in a hierarchical name, it needs to have a name by which external interfaces can refer to it. Each generate statement in a given scope is assigned a number even if it does not contain any unnamed generate blocks. The number will be 1 for the construct that appears textually first in that scope and will increase by 1 for each subsequent generate construct in that scope. All unnamed generate blocks will be given the name genblk<*n*> where <*n*> is the number assigned to its enclosing generate construct. If such a name would conflict with an explicitly declared name, then leading zeros are added in front of the number until the name does not conflict.

The following example demonstrates the use of hierarchical names in a top module with generate statements:

```
module top ();
    parameter genblk2 = 0;
    genvar i;

    // The following generate block is implicitly
    //   named genblk1

    if (genblk2) electrical a; // top.genblk1.a
    else          electrical b; // top.genblk1.b

    // The following generate block is implicitly
    // named genblk02 as genblk2 is already
    // a declared identifier

    if (genblk2) electrical a; // top.genblk02.a
    else electrical b; // top.genblk02.b

    // The following generate block would have been
    // named genblk3   but is explicitly named g1

    for (i = 0; i < 1; i = i + 1)
       begin : g1 // block name
          // The following generate block is
          // implicitly named genblk1 as the first
          //   nested scope inside of g1
          if (1) electrical a; // top.g1[0].genblk1.a
       end
```

```
// The following generate block is implicitly
// named genblk4 since it belongs to the fourth
// generate construct in scope "top".

// The previous generate block would have been
// named genblk3 if it had not been explicitly
// named g1

for (i = 0; i < 1; i = i + 1)

    // The following generate block is implicitly
    // named genblk1 as the first nested generate
    // block in genblk4

    if (1) electrical a;
      // top.genblk4[0].genblk1.a

    // The following generate block is implicitly
    // named genblk5
    if (1) electrical a; // top.genblk5.a
endmodule
```

Order of Elaboration

Elaboration is the process that occurs between parsing and simulation. It binds modules to module instances, builds the model hierarchy, computes parameter values, selects paramsets, resolves hierarchical names, establishes net connectivity, resolves disciplines and inserts connect modules, and prepares all of this for simulation. With the addition of generate statements, the order in which these tasks occur becomes significant. They are evaluated at elaboration time, and the result is determined before the simulation begins. Therefore, all expressions in generate schemes shall be constant expressions, deterministic at elaboration time.

If a generate statement contains an instantiation of an overloaded paramset, then the paramset selection is performed after the generate construct has been evaluated. The evaluation of the generate construct may influence the values and connections of the paramset instance, and hence the selection of matching paramset and module. The use of paramsets cannot introduce ambiguity as no `defparam` inside the hierarchy below a paramset instantiation is allowed.

Because of generate constructs and paramsets, the model hierarchy can depend on parameter values. Because defparam statements can alter parameter values from almost anywhere in the hierarchy, the result of elaboration can be ambiguous when generate constructs are involved. The final model hierarchy can depend on the order in which defparams and generate constructs are evaluated.

The following algorithm defines an order that produces the correct hierarchy:

1. A list of starting points is initialized with the list of top-level modules.

2. The hierarchy below each starting point is expanded as much as possible without elaborating generate constructs. All parameters encountered during this expansion are given their final values by applying initial values, parameter overrides, defparam statements, and paramset selections.

3. In other words, any defparam statement whose target can be resolved within the hierarchy elaborated so far must have its target resolved and its value applied. defparam statements whose target cannot be resolved are deferred until the next iteration of this step. Because no defparam

inside the hierarchy below a generate construct is
allowed to refer to a parameter outside the generate
construct, parameters can get their final values
before going to step 3.

4. Each generate construct encountered in step 2 is
    revisited, and the generate scheme is evaluated. The
    resulting generate block instantiations make up the
    new list of starting points. If the new list of starting
    points is not empty, go to step 2.

A module definition may have multiple analog blocks. The simulator
shall internally combine the multiple analog blocks into a single analog
block in the order that the analog blocks appear in the module description.
In other words, the analog blocks shall execute in the order that they are
specified in the module.

Concatenation of the analog blocks occurs after all generate statements
have been elaborated, that is, after the loop generate constructs have been
unrolled, and after the conditional generate constructs have been selected.
If an analog block appears in a loop generate statement, then the order
in which the loop is unrolled during elaboration determines the order in
which the analog blocks are concatenated to the eventual single analog
block after elaboration.

CHAPTER 19

Attributes

Verilog-A compilers and simulators often require additional information about specific objects within a Verilog-A code, beyond what is conveyed in the language itself. Attributes provide a mechanism for specifying such additional properties of various objects in the Verilog-A source and are left to be implemented by compilers that want to use them. Only standard Verilog-A attributes shall be implemented by compilers and simulators. Attributes may be used in various ways to control the creation of the executable model and model elaboration before the simulation. The concept of attributes is similar to *pragma* directives in programming languages, providing a hook to extra functionality in the language.

Introducing Attributes

An attribute is essentially defined by a name and a value associated with it. Attribute names are specified by identifier tokens while the values are basic type constants, associated with the attribute name by attribute assignments.

Attribute Assignments

The attribute assignments closely resemble the procedural assignments of Verilog-A variables using the syntax

```
attribute-name = constant-expressions
```

© Slobodan Mijalković 2022
S. Mijalković, *A Practical Guide to Verilog-A*, https://doi.org/10.1007/978-1-4842-6351-8_19

where *attribute-name* is an identifier. For example, the attribute assignments

```
channel = "N"
version = 503 + 1
revision = 1
```

associate string "N" and integers 504 and 1 with the attribute names channel, version, and revision, respectively. However, unlike procedural statements, attribute assignments do not end with a semicolon (;). Moreover, it is illegal to use a constant expression for attribute assignment if it contains the other attribute name:

```
version = 503 + revision // illegal
```

The identifiers representing attribute names are not declared and cannot be used in a Verilog-A procedural code. The attribute names and their associated values are only intended to be used by compilers in the preparation for the simulation but not during the simulation. For that reason, the attribute value must be only assigned to constant expressions, which can be determined before the actual simulation starts.

The constant expression defining attribute values can also contain parameters, as in the example:

```
memory_size = SIZE-1
```

where SIZE is a declared parameter. Since parameters can be redefined during model elaboration, it is possible to create in this way parameterized attributes that can be configured at the elaboration time.

The Verilog-A syntax allows specifying an attribute only by *attribute-name* without the equal sign (=) and an explicitly assigned value:

```
revision // the same as revision=1
```

In that case, the attributes are implicitly assigned to the integer value of 1. Such attributes could be particularly useful in the role of binary flags (true or false). The true value could be, for example, indicated by the attribute instantiation and the false value if the attribute is not instantiated.

Attribute Instances

Attribute instantiation associates attributes and their values with certain objects in the Verilog-A code to provide additional information to the compiler and simulation tool.

Attributes are instantiated in Verilog-A code by enclosing an attribute assignment within the token pair (* and *):

```
(* level = 504 *)
```

Multiple attributes can be instantiated within the same token pair (* and *) using a comma-separated list of attribute assignments:

```
(* level = 504, channel = "N" *)
```

It is equivalent to the instantiation of multiple attribute instances in a sequence:

```
(* level = 504 *) (* channel = "N" *)
```

The attribute instances can continue over many lines:

```
(* desc = "effective resistance",
   units = "Ohms",
   op = "yes",
   multiplicity = "divide" *)
*)
```

If the same attribute name is defined more than once, as in the example:

```
(* level = 504, channel = "N", level = 505 *)
```

the last attribute value shall be used and a simulation tool can give a warning that a duplicate attribute specification has occurred. Nesting of attribute instances:

```
(* level = 504, (* channel = "N" *) *) // error
```

is not allowed.

An attribute instance is always associated with just one specific object within a Verilog-A code. Some objects require to position attribute instances just before the object (as a prefix) while the other objects require to position attribute instances just after the object (as a suffix).

The objects that require attribute instantiation as a prefix are

- Declarations (modules, paramsets, user-defined functions, ports, nets, parameters, and variables)

- Module items (module instantiations and ports in port mappings, defparam statements, procedural and generable blocks and statements, event control statements)

Here are some examples of attaching attribute instances to declarations:

```
(* simplified *) module mosekv ( ... );

(* with_binning *) paramset nch nmos3;

(* distributed *) electrical [7:0] internal;

(* type="instance" *) parameter real w = 1.0e-4;

(* drain *) inout electrical d;
```

and module items:

```
(* long_channel *) mosekv
      mos1 (d, g, s, b, (* thermal_port *) dt);

(* override_1 *) defparam tgate.m1.gate_width = 5e-6;

(* initial_block *) initial begin ...

(* optional_nodes *)
if (nqsMod) begin : nqs
        electrical GP;
        electrical BP;
        ...
   end
```

An attribute can be associated as a prefix with a module declaration or an instance of that module. If an attribute has different values specified on both the module declaration and an instance of that module, the attribute on the instance will take precedence. If a net is also a module port, the attribute may also be specified on the port declaration line (in which the net is declared as input, inout, or output). If the attribute is specified for the same net identifier in both the net-discipline declaration and the port declaration, then the last attribute value shall be used and the tool can give a warning that a duplicate attribute specification has occurred.

Attributes are instantiated as a suffix to

- An operator or

- A call to a user-defined function

Here are some examples of attaching attribute instances as a prefix:

```
sum = a + (* second_argument *) b;

a = b ? (* no_glitch *) c : d;

maxValue (* smooth *) (val1, val2);
```

Besides being used in modules, attributes can be also associated with the parameters and variables in paramsets. The descriptive attributes in paramsets can be used by the simulator when generating help messages for the paramset.

When the compiler finds an attribute instance, the attribute names are examined to see if they are relevant for the executable model and simulator, and if it is, the attribute value is parsed and evaluated. If the attribute name is not recognized by a compiler, it is ignored, and in that case, an attribute instance is just another style of comment. However, the Verilog-A language introduces a set of standard attributes that shall be always processed by the Verilog-A compiler.

Standard Attributes

A set of standard attributes is defined in Verilog-A to support the creation of simulation reports. The simulator could use these attributes to generate detailed reports, help messages, and warnings on module interfaces, parameters, and variables using the standard attribute values. Standard attributes also allow designating some of the variables as output variables. The evolution of the output variable values is recorded during simulation similar to signal values. Finally, some of the recommended standard attributes are used to explicitly override module port disciplines.

Simulation Reports

The standard Verilog-A attributes introduced to support the simulation reports are given in Table 19-1.

Table 19-1. *The standard attributes supporting simulation reports*

Attribute	Role
desc	Description of the objects the attribute is attached to. It is used to generate help messages when attached to parameter, variable, and net declarations within a module. The attribute must be assigned a string
units	Describing the units of parameters or variables to which it is attached within a module. The attribute must be assigned a string
op	Indicating whether a parameter or variable should be included in a short report of the most useful operating point values. The attribute must be assigned a value, which must be either "yes" or "no"
multiplicity	Describing how the value of a parameter or variable should be scaled for reporting. The attribute must be assigned one of the following string values: "multiply", "divide", or "none"

The most common use of desc and units attributes is in module or paramset parameter declarations:

```
(* desc = "Resistance",
   units = "Ohms",
   op = "no",
   multiplicity = "none" *)
parameter real res = 1.0 from [0:inf);
```

Simulators can use the values of desc and units attributes for documentation purposes and when generating help messages for parameters. There is no dimensional analysis associated with the usage of the units attribute. However, it is often important for the user to know the units of a parameter, such as an angle that could be specified in radians or degrees. The units and desc attributes are of particular value for compact models, where the number of parameters is large and the description is not always clear from the parameter names.

If the multiplicity attribute is specified with the value "multiply" or "divide", the value for the associated parameter or variable will be multiplied or divided by the value of $mfactor in any report of operating point values. If the multiplicity attribute is not specified or specified with the value "none", then no scaling will be performed in the operating point reports.

Note   The scaling defined by the multiplicity attribute applies to operating point value reports; it does not affect the automatic scaling of variables and parameters with hierarchical system parameters.

The desc attribute can be also attached to net declarations:

```
(* desc="drain terminal" *) electrical d;
```

This information can be used by the simulator to generate descriptive help messages related to the usage of nets.

The standard attributes desc and units have a special meaning when attached to module and paramset variables annotating them as output variables.

Output Variables

The variables associated with a desc or units attribute, or both, shall be known as output variables. For example, the following declarations:

```
(* desc="gate-source capacitance", units="F" *)
real cgs;

(* desc="effective resistance", units="Ohms"
   op="yes",  multiplicity="divide" *) real reff;
```

define the variables cgs and reff as output variables. The simulators shall provide access to their values during simulation in a similar way the signal values are accessible. Besides printing the names, values, units, and descriptions of output variables in simulation reports, the output variables are also available for plotting as a function of time or the swept variable of a DC sweep along with the net signals.

Note   The units and desc attributes have a special meaning only for variables with global (module or paramset) scope. The units and desc attributes for block-level variables in modules shall be ignored by the simulator, but can be still used for code documentation purposes.

The standard attributes desc and units can be also used to annotate output variables in paramsets. A few special rules apply to paramset output variables and output variables of modules referenced by a paramset:

- If a paramset output variable has the same name as an output variable of the module, the value of the paramset output variable is the value reported for any instance that uses the paramset.

- If a paramset variable without a description has the same name as an output variable of the module, the module output variable of that name shall not be available for instances that use the paramset.

A paramset output variable's value may be computed from values of paramset parameters and local variables as well as any output variable of the module. The module output variables are accessed using the hierarchical reference:

. module-output-variable-name

The following example declares an output variable ft for instances of the paramset smnpn:

```
paramset smnpn npn;
  (* desc="cut-off frequency" *) real ft;
  .is=2.0e-17; .bf=120.0; .br=10; rb=145;
  .rc=75; .re=12;
  .cje=2.0e-14; .vje=0.9; .mje=0.4;
  .cjc=3.0e-14; .vjc=0.6; .mjc=0.3; .xcjc=0.2;
  ft = .gm/('M_TWO_PI*(.cpi + .cmu));
endparamset
```

The module npn is assumed to have output variables named gm, cpi, and cmu. If the module npn had an output variable named ft, the paramset's output variable would replace it.

Port Discipline Override

The attribute port_discipline is used to define the desired discipline for ports it is attached to. The attribute value shall be a string and the value must be a valid Verilog-A discipline. It can be attached to a model instance:

```
(* port_discipline = "electrical" *)
resistor #(.r(1k)) r1 (node1, node2); // not needed as default

(* port_discipline = "rotational" *)
      resistor #(.r(1k)) r2 (node1, node2);
```

to change the basic discipline of all ports for the module instance. It can be also attached to the particular port of the module instance:

```
resistor #(.r(1k)) r3
        ((* port_discipline="rotational" *) node1,
        (* port_discipline="rotational" *) node2);
```

to override a discipline for the specific ports. The use of these attributes can be combined to change the basic discipline of all ports for the module instance, but override the discipline for specific ports. The following provides an example of this use:

```
(* port_discipline="electrical" *) vcvs
   #(.gain(1.45e-3)) motor1 (n1, gnd_e,
   (* port_discipline="rotational_omega" *) shaft1,
   (* port_discipline="rotational_omega" *) gnd_rot);
```

The preceding model uses a voltage-controlled voltage source to model a motor as a converter from electrical potential to rotational velocity.

If the attribute port_discipline is not found attached to the module instance or ports, then the module ports will acquire the disciplines of other nets connected to module ports. If no disciplines are connected to that nets, then the default discipline is set to electrical.

CHAPTER 20

Compiler Directives

Compiler directives control the preprocessor part of Verilog-A compilation. These directives are capable of performing various transformations on the Verilog-A code but know nothing about the Verilog-A syntax and simply make textual changes as directed. It typically involves the inclusion of the text files, substitution of strings, conditional inclusion or exclusion of code, and setting defaults. The scope of a compiler directive is independent of module definitions and extends from the point where the directive occurs to the next compiler directive that supersedes it.

The Verilog-A compiler directives are preceded by the (`) character (grave accent) which should not be confused with the apostrophe character ('). Whitespace characters can precede the directive but more than one directive on the same line is not permitted. Verilog-A offers a multitude of standard compiler directives to steer the source of your code.

File Inclusion

Verilog-A code can be organized into different files and then compiled together as one unit. One of the useful features for gathering Verilog-A source code fragments into a single compilation unit is the include compiler directive. It takes the form

```
`include "filename"
```

© Slobodan Mijalković 2022
S. Mijalković, *A Practical Guide to Verilog-A*, https://doi.org/10.1007/978-1-4842-6351-8_20

It instructs the preprocessor to insert the content of the file, whose name is identified by *filename*, in the code at the point where the include compiler directive appears.

The `include directive can be specified anywhere within the Verilog-A description. Only whitespace or comment may appear on the same line with the `include directive. A file included in the source using the `include directive may contain other `include compiler directives. Compiler implementation may limit the maximum number of nesting levels for including files.

The whitespace is significant within the double quote characters of the `include directive. An include directive

```
`include " fileA.inc   "
```

will not find the required fileA.inc. The *filename* must be the name of an existing file that may optionally be preceded by a full or relative directory path specification. The syntax of directory path specifications depends on the operating system on which the Verilog-A code is compiled. For example, the include directive

```
`include "../noise.va"
```

on the Linux operating systems will be replaced during compilation by the file noise.va located in the parent directory. An included file may itself contain compiler directives.

The `include directive is particularly useful when used for the inclusion of the standard definitions of natures, disciplines, and physical constants:[1]

```
`include "disciplines.vams"
`include "constants.vams"
```

---

[1] www.accellera.org/downloads/standards/v-ams

In all the Verilog-A code presented in the previous chapters, we have implicitly assumed the inclusion of the standard natures and disciplines and optionally the definition of the physical constants.

Macro Definition

A macro (short for "macro instruction") is a fragment of code that has been given a name. Whenever the name is used, it is replaced by the content of macro. Macros can be defined and used both inside and outside module definitions. There are two kinds of macros: object-like and function-like macros.

Object-like Macros

An object-like macro is defined by using the syntax:

`` `define `` *macro-name macro-text*

where the `` `define `` compiler directive is followed by an identifier *macro-name*, introducing a name of the macro, and then a sequence of token *macro-text* that should act as a replacement for the macro name. The *macro-text* can be also blank, in which case the macro is defined to be empty and no text is substituted when the macro is used.

If more than one line is necessary to specify *macro-text*, it can be continued onto several lines by placing a backslash (\) character, without trailing spaces, at the end of each line to be continued. The macro will be expanded as a multiline text but without backslash characters. If a one-line comment is included in the *macro-text*, then the comment shall not become part of the substituted text.

The compiler shall substitute any occurrence of the token `` `macro-name `` in the source description with the *macro-text*. The scope of the defined macro name is from the point of its definition to the end of the source file being compiled. The token `macro-name can be used anywhere in the source description. However, it shall not be split across the lexical tokens.

A macro definition can use previous macro definitions. It shall be an error for a macro to expand text containing another usage of itself (a recursive macro). Basically, all compiler directives shall be considered as being predefined macros. However, redefining a compiler directive as a macro name is illegal.

Object-like macros are conventionally used as part of good programming practice to create symbolic names for numeric constants:

```
`define SPEED_OF_LIGHT 2.997925e8
`define PI 3.141592653
```

It is common, but not obligatory, to use uppercase letters for constants to distinguish them from the variables. Such definitions have no runtime overhead during the simulation and increase the readability of the Verilog-A code.

Function-like Macros

A function-like macro is defined by using the syntax:

```
`define macro-name ( formal-argument, ... ) macro-text
```

It is similar to the definition of the object-like macros, except for the comma-separated list of *formal-argument* identifiers in parentheses after the *macro-name*. The *formal-argument* can be any valid Verilog-A simple identifier. Such a macro definition looks like a function call and the function-like macros basically act like functions but without the associated calling overhead.

The preprocessor searches subsequent lines for occurrences of the macro "call":

```
`macro-name ( actual-argument, ... )
```

where each *formal-argument* is now substituted by an *actual-argument*, which can be any valid Verilog-A expression. The number of actual arguments must match the number of formal arguments in the macro definition. When the macro is expanded, each use of a formal argument in its *macro-text* is replaced by tokens of the corresponding *actual-argument*.

For example, a macro definition

```
`define MAX(A, B) ((A) > (B) ? (A) : (B))
```

used in a subsequent statement as

```
y = `MAX(p+q, r+s);
```

will be replaced by the line

```
y = ((p+q) > (r+s) ? (p+q) : (r+s));
```

Note the excessive use of parentheses here because macros perform purely textual substitution and, without these parentheses, unexpected expansions may take place. For instance, a macro definition

```
`define SQUARE(X) (X * X)
y = `SQUARE(u+v);
```

is equivalent to

```
y = (u + v * u + v);
```

which is very different from intended

```
y = (u + v) * (u + v);
```

The function-like macros are often used to replace the user-defined functions. For example, the following user-defined function definition and a calling statement:

```
analog function real hypsmooth;
    input x,c;
```

```
    real x, c;
    begin
        hypsmooth = 0.5*(x+sqrt(x*x + 4.0*c*c);
    end
endfunction
...
t3 = hypsmooth(t1-t2, -1.0E-6)
```

can be replaced with macro definition and expansion:

```
`define hypsmooth (x, c) \
    (0.5*((x)+sqrt((x)*(x) + 4.0*(c)*(c))))
...
t3 = `hypsmooth(t1-t2, -1.0E-6)
```

The use of functions is safer since the compiler can check the function argument types. The main benefit of using macros instead of functions could be a faster execution time. During preprocessing, a macro is expanded (replaced by its definition) inline each time.

Undefining Macros

A previously defined macro name can be undefined using the `undef compiler directive as

```
`undef macro-name
```

It tells the preprocessor to remove all definitions for the specified *macro-name*. An attempt to undefine a macro that was not previously defined using the `define directive can result in a warning. An undefined macro has no value, just as it had never been defined.

Predefined Macros

Verilog-A standards and simulators can also provide predefined macros that can be used to include or exclude portions of the code specific to a particular Verilog-A version or simulator. To avoid conflicts with the predefined Verilog-A macros, the user-defined macros shall never begin with __VAMS_ which is reserved for the predefined macros. The `define compiler directive shall not affect predefined macros and the simulator may issue a warning for an attempt to undefine predefined macros.

The Verilog-A LRM 2.2 introduced a number of extensions to support compact modeling and also the predefined object-like macro:

```
__VAMS_COMPACT_MODELING__
```

It is implicitly defined by the compiler if and only if all the compact modeling extensions from LRM 2.2 are supported by the simulator. It allows to conditionally compile the code with the compact modeling extensions if they are supported or to generate warnings or errors if they are not.

Conditional Compilation

It is often convenient to be able to have multiple versions of the same code. It can be achieved by `ifdef, `ifndef, `elsif, `else, and `endif compiler directives for the conditional compilation. They work together in two sequences of directives, the ifdef-sequence:

```
`ifdef macro-name code-fragment
`elsif macro-name code-fragment
...
`else code-code fragment
`endif
```

introduced with the `` `ifdef `` directive, and the ifndef-sequence:

```
`ifndef macro-name code-fragment
`elsif macro-name code-fragment
...
`else code-fragment
`endif
```

introduced with the `` `ifndef `` directive. The `` `endif `` directive signifies the end of the conditional sequences. There cannot be more than one `` `else `` directive (there may be none) in a sequence, although there may be any number (including zero) of `` `elsif `` directives preceding the `` `else `` directive. Each of the directives in the sequence (except `` `endif ``) is associated with a code fragment, but only one or none of the code fragments will be compiled based on the definition status of *macro-name* identifiers in `` `ifdef ``, `` `ifndef ``, and `` `elsif `` directives.

The definition status of *macro-name* identifiers is tested sequentially starting from the `` `ifdef `` or `` `ifndef `` directive. The code fragment of the first directive in a sequence returning the true condition will be compiled, ignoring the remaining directives. If the true condition is not found, and there is an `` `else `` directive in the sequence, the `` `else `` code fragment will be compiled; otherwise, none of the code fragments will be compiled.

Nesting of compiler directives for conditional compilation is permitted, as it is illustrated in the following example:

```
`ifdef wow
   $display("wow is defined");
   `ifdef nest_one
     $display("nest_one is defined");
     `ifdef nest_two
       $display("nest_two is defined");
     `else
       $display("nest_two is not defined");
     `endif
```

```
`else
    $display("nest_one is not defined");
  `endif
`else
    $display("wow is not defined");
    `ifdef second_nest
      $display("second_nest is defined");
    `else
      $display("second_nest is not defined");
    `endif
`endif
```

The conditional compilation directives are used in the standard nature definitions, as shown in the following example of the Current nature definition:

```
nature Current;
  units        = "A";
  access       = I;
  idt_nature   = Charge;
`ifdef CURRENT_ABSTOL
  abstol       = `CURRENT_ABSTOL;
`else
  abstol       = 1e-12;
`endif
endnature
```

It allows redefining the value of the nature abstol attribute by the user-defined object-like macro CURRENT_ABSTOL.

The following example illustrates the usage of the predefined macro:

```
`ifdef __VAMS_COMPACT_MODELING__
    reff = ddx(iab, V(a));
```

```
    I(a,b) <+ white_noise(4.0 * 'P_K *
            $temperature * reff, "thermal");
`else
    if (analysis("noise"))
        $strobe("Noise not computed.");
`endif
```

The noise of a nonlinear resistor is evaluated and contributed only if the compiler supports the use of the derivative operator ddx() introduced as one of the compact modeling–related language extensions in Verilog-A LRM 2.2.

Default Transition Directive

This directive specifies the default value for rise and fall times for the transition filter introduced in Chapter 14. The syntax for this directive is

```
`default_transition transition-time
```

where *transition-time* is a real value.

For all transition filters which follow a default transition directive and do not have rise time and fall time arguments specified, *transition-time* is used for their default rise and fall time values. If another `default_transition directive is encountered in the subsequent source description, the transition filters following the newly encountered directive derive their default rise and fall times from the transition time value of the newly encountered directive. In other words, the default rise and fall times for a transition filter are derived from the *transition-time* value of the directive which immediately precedes the transition filter. If a default transition directive is not used in the description, *transition-time* is controlled by the simulator as described in Chapter 14.

APPENDIX

Reserved Words in Verilog-A
Keywords

above	abs	absdelay
absdelta	abstol	acos
acosh	ac_stim	aliasparam
analog	analysis	asin
asinh	atan	atan2
atanh	begin	branch
case	ceil	continuous
cos	cosh	cross
ddt	ddt_nature	ddx
defpar	discipline	else
end	endcase	enddiscipline
endfunction	endgenerate	endmodule
endnature	endparamset	endtable
exclude	exp	final_step
flicker_noise	floor	flow
for	from	function
generate	genvar	ground
hypot	idt	idtmod

(*continued*)

© Slobodan Mijalković 2022
S. Mijalković, *A Practical Guide to Verilog-A*, https://doi.org/10.1007/978-1-4842-6351-8

idt_nature	if	inf
initial_step	inout	input
integer	laplace_nd	laplace_np
laplace_zd	laplace_zp	last_crossing
limexp	ln	localparam
log	macromodule	max
min	module	nature
negedge	noise_table	noise_table_log
or	output	parameter
paramset	potential	pow
real	sin	sinh
slew	sqrt	string
table	tan	tanh
timer	transition	units
while	white_noise	zi_nd
zi_np	zi_zd	zi_zp

Other Reserved Words

access	always	and
assert	assign	automatic
buf	bufif0	bufif1
casex	casez	cell
cmos	config	connect

(*continued*)

connectmodule	connectrules	deassign
default	design	disable
discrete	domain	driver_update
edge	endconfig	endconnectrules
endprimitive	endspecify	endtask
event	force	forever
fork	highz0	highz1
ifnone	incdir	include
initial	instance	join
large	liblist	library
medium	merged	nand
net_resolution	nmos	nor
noshowcancelled	not	notif0
notif1	pmos	primitive
pull0	pull1	pulldown
pullup	pulsestyle_onevent	pulsestyle_ondetect
rcmos	realtime	reg
release	repeat	resolveto
rnmos	rpmos	rtran
rtranif0	rtranif1	scalared
showcancelled	signed	small
specify	specparam	split
strong0	strong1	supply0
supply1	task	time

(continued)

tran	tranif0	tranif1
tri	tri0	tri1
triand	trior	trireg
unsigned	use	uwire
vectored	wait	wand
weak0	weak1	wire
wor	wreal	xnor
xor		

SPICE Compatibility

Table A-1. *Names for primitives, parameters, and ports in SPICE*

Primitive Name	Port Names	Parameter Names
resistor	p, n	r, tc1, tc2
capacitor	p, n	c, ic
inductor	p, n	l, ic
iexp	p, n	dc, mag, phase, val0, val1, td0, tau0, td1, tau1
ipulse	p, n	dc, mag, phase, val0, val1, td, rise, fall, width, period
ipwl	p, n	dc, mag, phase, wave

(*continued*)

Table A-1. (*continued*)

Primitive Name	Port Names	Parameter Names
isine	p, n	dc, mag, phase, offset, ampl, freq, td, damp, sinephase, ammodindex, ammodfreq, ammodphase, fmmodindex, fmmodfreq
vexp	p, n	dc, mag, phase, val0, val1, td0, tau0, td1, tau1
vpulse	p,n	dc, mag, phase, val0,val1, td, rise, fall,width, period
vpwl	p, n	dc, mag, phase, wave
vsine	p, n	dc, mag, phase, offset, ampl, freq, td, damp, sinephase, ammodindex, ammodfreq, ammodphase, fmmodindex, fmmodfreq
tline	t1, b1, t2, b2	z0, td, f, nl
vccs	sink, src,ps, ns	gm
vcvs	p, n, ps, ns	gain
diode	a, c	area
bjt	c, b, e, s	area
mosfet	d, g, s, b	w, l, ad, as, pd, ps, nrd, nrs
jfet	d, g, s	area
msfet	d, g, s	area

Index

A

Above() function, 224, 225
Absolute delay filter, 201, 202
Accelerometer, 147–149
AC transfer function, 204
Actual argument reference, 173
Actual port declarations, 55
Analog function, 165
Analog function real
        hypsmooth, 168
Analysis() function, 233
Analysis types, 232
Argument association, 171
Arithmetic expressions, 22, 23
Array, 174
arrayadd function, 169
Array assignments, 105, 106
Array parameters, 31, 71
Array variables, 31, 98, 99, 167
Assignment pattern, 30, 31, 50, 71,
        100, 172, 174, 183, 207
Assignment statement, 103
   array assignment, 105, 106
   scalar assignments, 104, 105
Attributes, 281, 291
   assignments, 281
   comma-separated list, 283

concept, 281
constant expression, 282
declarations, 284
instantiation, 283, 284
model and simulator, 286
modules, 285, 286
multiplicity, 288
simulation tool, 284
standard, 286, 288
suffix, 285

B

Base format tokens, 9
Base natures, 34–37, 46
Basic types, Verilog-A language, 17
   integer type, 17, 18
   real types, 18, 19
   string types, 19
Bitwise expressions, 25, 26
Bounding time step, 241
Branch
   definition, 115
   port branches, 119, 120
   scalar branches, 115, 116
   vector branches, 117–119
Branch-reference, 122, 126

© Slobodan Mijalković 2022
S. Mijalković, *A Practical Guide to Verilog-A*, https://doi.org/10.1007/978-1-4842-6351-8

W, X, Y

Z

Printed in the United States
by Baker & Taylor Publisher Services